THE BAT

THE BAT

Wings in the Night Sky

M. BROCK FENTON

FIREFLY BOOKS

A FIREFLY BOOK

Cataloguing in Publication Data

Fenton, M. Brock (Melville Brockett), 1943–
   Bat: wings in the night sky

Includes bibliographical references.
ISBN 1-55209-253-4

1. Bats. I. Title

QL737.C5F445 1998a   599.4   C98-930376-4

Published in Canada in 1998 by Key Porter Books Limited.

Published in the United States in 1998
by Firefly Books (U.S.) Inc.
P.O. Box 1338
Ellicott Station
Buffalo, New York, USA
14205

Principal photography: M. Brock Fenton
Design: Scott Richardson
Electronic formatting: Jean Lightfoot Peters
Illustration on p. 129: Sylvie Bouchard

Printed and bound in Italy

98 99 00 01 6 5 4 3 2 1

Page 1: Hemprich's big-eared bat.

Page 3: This 7-gram fringed myotis is poised for take-off. These insectivorous bats occur in the western United States and in southern British Columbia.

C O N T E N T S

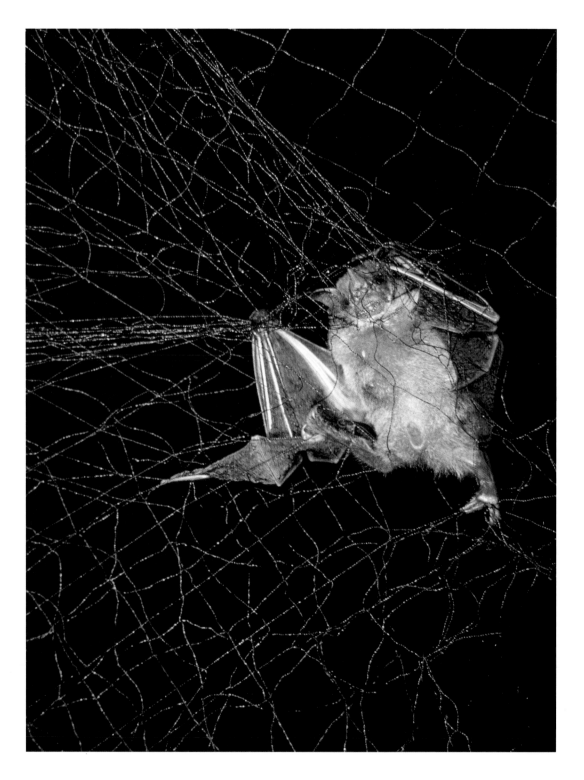

Bats do make mistakes. This yellow-shouldered bat is tangled in a mist net, which it normally would have seen or detected with its echolocation.

ONE

THE LURE OF BATS

This roosting pygmy fruit bat hangs from one foot, while enveloping its body with its wings.

Bats are different from other mammals! Sometimes it's their wings that make the difference so obvious to an observer. Or it may be the fact that many bats hang upside down that makes them seem so very different from us. People wonder about bats that hang upside down and whether all of their blood must rush to their heads. It would be just as reasonable for bats to assume that when we stand the blood will rush to our feet. (It could be worse when we sit down.) The same kinds of mechanisms that allow us to stand without having the blood rush to our feet protect hanging bats, as well as the giraffe that bends over to get a drink.

Bats are different from people in interesting ways. For a start they are nocturnal. This means that we rarely encounter them and, when we do, they can

A flying little brown bat shows off the basic structure of the Chiroptera—wings that are folds of skin supported by elongated arm, forearm, hand, and finger bones. The wing membranes attach to the hind legs and the side of the body and envelop the tail. Little brown bats are insectivorous and occur widely in North America.

make a strong impression on us. I still remember the first live bat that I met. It was August 1951 at a cottage near Orillia, Ontario. The bats that lived behind the shutters on the cottage next door had been disturbed by painters. They flew away and one of them found its way into our cottage. Inside the cottage, the bat landed on the stone mantel. When I grabbed it, going low to avoid the head, I was immediately bitten. In this way I learned that bats hang upside down. The bat had bitten me in self-defense, but it was too small to break the skin and none of us worried about the possibility that it might have been rabid.

Why do bats hang upside down? I suspect that this posture reflects the fact that their forelimbs are wings, which makes their arms and hands proportionally very large. The arrangement and structure of the tendons in a bat's hind foot means that hanging does not involve the contraction of any muscles. Thus it does not cost a bat to hang as it does us to stand. Furthermore, as every hang-glider knows, it's easier to take off from a height, and perhaps easier still when you start from an upside-down position. However, not all bats hang upside down. The bats that hang and do not crawl or run have rather spindly hind legs, while species that are more active on the ground, like common vampire bats and free-tailed bats, have bigger thigh bones.

Another astonishing feature of bats is their small size. In September 1995, Canada Post issued a forty-five-cent stamp that depicted a flying hoary bat. At the time, the stamp, one of four designed to recognize animals that migrated from Canada to Mexico, was enough postage to send a hoary bat anywhere in Canada by mail (provided that the address and

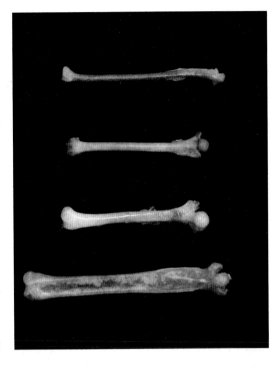

The thigh bones of a common vampire bat (bottom) and a Malaysian free-tailed bat (directly above) are much more robust than those of a Geoffroy's horseshoe bat (top) or a big brown bat (directly below). Common vampire bats and Malaysian free-tailed bats are very active on the ground. Geoffroy's horseshoe bats are almost immobile on the ground, and their spindly thighs reflect their roosting posture (hanging upside down). Big brown bats are intermediate between the other extremes and have thigh bones of modest proportions.

On stamp: CANADA *migratory wildlife* *faune migratrice* MÉXICO

Hoary Bat
Chauve-souris cendrée

Canada 45

A 1995 Canadian postage stamp depicting a flying hoary bat attacking a moth.

postal code were correct). At 30 grams, hoary bats are the largest bats that occur in Canada, but they weigh no more than the envelope containing your telephone bill. In linear dimensions hoary bats may seem bigger (wingspan of 40 cm), but flying animals need large wings to support their weight.

The smallest bats in Canada are eastern or western small-footed bats at body weights of around 4 grams and wingspans of about 23 centimetres. The smallest bats in the world, the bumblebee bats of Thailand, weigh only about 2 grams and would feel the same in your hand as a dime. The largest bats in the world, gigantic flying foxes, can weigh as much as 1,500 grams and have wingspans of up to 2 meters. To get a clearer picture of just how small bats really are, compare the weight of the largest bat to your own weight, let alone that of an African elephant (5,443,000 grams) or that of a blue whale (182,000,000 grams).

Like people, elephants, and whales, bats are mammals. Female bats give birth to live young and feed them milk. Newborn bats are huge compared to the young of these other mammals. An 8-gram little brown bat gives birth to a baby that weighs about 2 grams (25 percent of her weight). Newborn humans usually weigh 3,000 to 3,600 grams (6 percent of the mother's weight). The newborn African elephant weighs just 3 percent of its mother's weight, the blue whale 1 percent.

Also like humans, elephants, and whales, bats usually just have one young at a time, although some species, such as big brown bats in eastern North America, often bear twins. While we expect larger mammals like humans, elephants, and whales to live a long time, people are surprised to learn that this also is true of some bats. By placing numbered bands on the wings of bats, biologists have learned that the Methuselahs of the bat world are little brown bats and greater horseshoe bats. In eastern Ontario, one banded little brown bat is known to have lived over thirty years

A roosting hoary bat, the largest species that occurs in Canada. These bats roost in foliage and make extensive migrations.

A female Wood's slit-faced bat with her newborn baby roosts under the roof of an open-air kitchen in Kruger National Park, South Africa. This insectivorous bat also roosts in hollow trees and in caves.

in the wild, while in the southwest of England some banded greater horseshoe bats also have passed the thirty-year mark.

By banding bats we have learned that some of them make lengthy migrations. In Europe, for example, noctules banded in the north of Germany have been found farther south, and in Australia, bent-winged bats may regularly travel hundreds of kilometers between their summer and winter roosts. The

Schreiber's bent-winged bat (10 grams) is an insectivorous species that occurs from southern Europe through Africa and out to Australia. This plain-nosed bat lacks the facial ornamentation that is typical of some other bats.

The doglike features of this Egyptian fruit bat (120 grams) reflect its classification with "flying foxes," the fruit bats of the Old World tropics (Africa, India, Southeast Asia, and Australia).

same is true of little brown bats in North America, which do not just fly south for the winter. Little brown bats migrate to a hibernation site which may be north, east, south, or west of their summer haunts.

We think that some hoary bats make even more spectacular migrations of thousands of kilometers, between their summer range in Canada and their winter grounds much farther south. By placing colored bands on the wings of hoary bats captured in southwestern Ontario, some of my students found that some individuals returned year after year to the same feeding sites. (We never did find out where these tagged bats spent the winter.)

Bats' wings are folds of skin supported by elongated arm, forearm, hand,

A little sac-winged bat (8 grams), a sheath-tailed bat from Central and South America, hunts flying insects which it detects, tracks, and assesses by echolocation. Note the large eyes and the flexible snout.

and finger bones, essentially like the bones of a human arm and hand. The wings attach to the sides of the body and to the hind legs. In many species, the wing membranes are continuous with membranes that join the hind feet and enclose the tail. Specifically, fingers two, three, four, and five support the wing, while the thumb, digit one, is relatively free (although some bats have a membrane in front of the upper arm and forearm).

Bats reflexively fold up their wings when they land, and some species envelop their bodies in their wings when roosting. Although the wing membranes of bats are relatively flexible and resilient, they can be torn or punctured. Fortunately, the membranes heal relatively quickly and thus bats can withstand some wear and tear on them. Most large slit-faced bats that I have seen have scars on their wing membranes, suggesting that punctures and tears may be a regular occurrence. While some bats survive some damage to their

wing membranes, the supporting bones are more essential. I have found bats with finger and hand bones that have been broken and healed, but I have never seen a wild bat that has survived a broken upper arm or forearm.

The variety of bats is impressive. Although their basic design is typical of mammals (warm blood, teeth, bearing live young who feed on milk), there are over 900 living species of bats in the world. Most of these species inhabit tropical and subtropical areas. For example, although there are 19 species of bats that occur regularly in Canada, and 14 species in the United Kingdom, there are at least 80 species in Mexico and over 65 species in Zimbabwe.

Some of this variety is reflected in the faces of different bats. Another indication of the diversity of bats comes in their diet (see "What Bats Eat") and the variety of places where they roost by day (see "Surviving the Day: Where Bats Roost").

What makes us curious about bats? Being bitten at an early age may explain my fascination, although it lay dormant for twelve years until December 1963, when I visited my first bat cave. The cave was located near Kingston, Ontario, in "the hell holes," an area of karst topography along the Salmon River. My visions of immense caverns and miles of passages were toned down by the reality of short passages that were chest-high and narrow. My hope for thousands of bats resolved into two northern long-eared bats that hung from the ceiling in hibernation, just above a porcupine that bristled with indignation at the disturbance. The bats were coated with droplets of water and appeared to be deeply asleep. On the same trip other caves provided larger passages and a few more bats.

For me the lure of bats is rather like the lure of caves. There is always the prospect of discovering something new. In those days, one of my dreams was finding a bat that someone had banded elsewhere to document its movement from one place to another. Another was just to find a cave or an old mine that was "full of bats" to help us learn just where the local bats went for the winter.

Leaflike structures dominate the faces of many species of bats, but few are as spectacular as Tome's long-eared bat (15 grams), an insectivorous, New World leaf-nosed bat.

At first I may have been a bit confused about which was more exciting, the bats or the caves. It didn't take long for the bats to take over.

Some dreams do come true. By 1964 I had been shown a cave with some hibernating bats in it, one that was not known previously to other bat banders. Then, in May 1965, I first visited an abandoned mine near Renfrew, a hibernation site for thousands of bats. Both sites were the focus of my work over the next five years. In June 1966 in the attic of a farmhouse near Lyndhurst, Ontario, I found a bat that had been banded while hibernating in an abandoned mine on the west side of Lake Champlain in New York State. The real excitement of bats, the lure of these creatures, is the combination of their diversity and our ignorance. Bats offer biologists many rich opportunities for study.

Bats also present opportunities for other animals. Although they are small, and for many predators hardly bite-sized, bats can be an important source of food. In Kruger National Park in South Africa, little free-tailed bats often roost in large numbers in the attics of buildings and in the expansion joints on bridges. Around dusk, the bats emerge to hunt their insect prey, and on many nights several different kinds of birds of prey converge on big bat roosts to harvest the bats. The same kind of scene plays itself out every night when large numbers of bats emerge. The important point for the predator is the concentration of bats, provided there is time to catch and eat enough of them as they leave.

At the high water bridge over the Letaba River in Kruger National Park, Wahlberg's eagles, African goshawks, and hobby falcons regularly hunt the little free-tailed bats that live in the bridge. There are usually thousands of bats. I have watched a pair of Wahlberg's eagles arrive about twenty minutes before the first bats leave the bridge. The eagles sit patiently on tree branches on either side of the bridge to wait for the bats. The African goshawks do the same thing, while the hobby falcons fly back and forth overhead.

The first bats to emerge signal the eagles and the goshawks to take flight. While the bats leaving the bridge fly up or downstream, the birds work across the valley, gaining some altitude and then diving to try to catch a bat.

Brock Fenton exploring a cave near Belleville, Ontario, in 1963. Photograph by the late R. E. Beschel.

Wahlberg's eagles succeed on about half of their attacks. The goshawks and the eagles take their captured bat to a perch to eat it, taking as little as thirty seconds from the time of capture until they are airborne and hunting again. The birds usually have only twenty minutes to hunt the bats because as soon as it gets dark they leave, even though bats continue to emerge from the roosts. The eagles, the goshawks, and the falcons do not see well in the dark, so that on a good night one eagle might catch only twenty bats (enough energy to fuel the bird for a day).

The birds have learned how to exploit the bats. But why would the bats not wait twenty minutes before emerging from their roosts? By postponing their departure the bats could entirely avoid the Wahlberg's eagles, the African goshawks, and the hobby falcons. The dusk abundance of insects and/or the pressure of having to forage in competition with so many other colony members could explain the bats' risk-prone behavior. Certainly, the more bats that emerge from a roost at the same time, the less risk there is to any one bat.

Birds hunting bats raises interesting questions about the behavior of the bats and the birds. Why are bats nocturnal? I can think of at least four reasons, and all of them could apply. First, vulnerability to birds that hunt by day and to other predators could be one pressure that has led bats to be nocturnal. Second, day-flying bats may be prone to overheating when they fly in the sun, making nocturnal behavior a sensible alternative. Third, for bats that hunt flying insects, birds such as swifts and swallows may be significant competition. Fourth, if the ancestors of bats were nocturnal, the habit stuck. In other words, we don't know why bats are nocturnal, and it remains for some imaginative biologist to design an experiment that will help us to choose between alternatives.

Bats are captivating for a number of reasons. First, many of them are high tech marvels, depending upon their acute sense of hearing and extraordinary sense of timing to "echolocate." This behavior involves animals using echoes of sounds they have produced to locate objects in their path. This "biosonar," mistakenly called "radar," is an extraordinary behavior that serves many (but not all) bats in a variety of ways. Second, bats are the original opportunists, whether the topic is finding a place to spend the day or finding something to eat. People find roosting bats in the most astonishing places, from under stones to the spaces behind window shutters. Bats are very catholic in their tastes, with some species eating everything from leaves to fruit, flowers to insects and fish, to other bats.

TWO

BATS CAN SEE WITH THEIR EARS!

The eyes of this California leaf-nosed bat (10 grams) are much less conspicuous than those of the owl. These insectivorous bats see very well, particularly in dim lighting.

Bats are shrouded in mystery. Learning about bats and solving their mysteries can begin with a question. How do bats fly at night and avoid crashing into things? How do flying bats detect obstacles? A clue is provided by the fact that most bats fly with their mouths open.

In the 1780s, the Italian scientist Lazarro Spallanzani asked this question, comparing the flight performances of bats and owls. He found that at night in a room lighted only by a candle, both bats and owls flew about and did not bump into the furniture or the walls. Blowing out the candle changed the situation. Now the owls were reluctant to fly, while the bats flew readily. When forced to fly, the owls collided with obstacles that the flying bats avoided.

These results could suggest that bats had more effective vision than owls,

In 1980, Donald R. Griffin tends a mist net set to catch echolocating swiftlets (birds) as they emerged from Christmas Pot, a cave near Chillagoe, Queensland, Australia.

a conclusion not obvious from the appearances of these animals. While the eyes dominate the face of an owl, they are much less conspicuous in bats. To test the explanation of differences in visual performance, Spallanzani blinded his experimental bats and owls.

The sightless owls and bats behaved the same as they had in the dark room before being blinded. Owls clearly differed from bats. Spallanzani then performed experiments that denied the bats their use of touch and their sense of smell. Neither experiment changed the behavior of the blinded bats. But when he put a bat's head into a sack or blocked one of its ears, Spallanzani could finally disorient it. He concluded that bats could "see" with their ears.

In 1790 this suggestion was considered preposterous because everyone "knew" that animals did not see with their ears. Spallanzani's "bat problem" went on record as one of those unexplained mysteries. The story illustrates how science proceeds: from a question to experiments, to more questions and more experiments. It also demonstrates how resistant people, including other scientists, can be to suggestions that are beyond their imagination.

In the late 1930s, the American zoologist Donald R. Griffin coined the

Large, conspicuous eyes dominate the face of this spotted eagle owl, which is widespread in Africa.

term *echolocation* and resolved Spallanzani's bat problem. Griffin showed how little brown bats used *echoes* of sounds they produced to *locate* objects in their path. Griffin repeated some of Spallanzani's experiments and added others of his own design. He monitored the bats' behavior with a "sonic detector," an instrument sensitive to sound beyond the range of human hearing. As the bats flew around a room they produced pulses of ultrasonic sound at frequencies (pitch) above 20 kilohertz (kHz), which is by definition beyond our hearing range.

What is necessary for echolocation? *Time* is one critical element. By measuring the time it takes for the pulse of sound to travel to a target and back, the bat determines its distance from (range to) the object. Sound travels about

The echolocation calls of Noack's leaf-nosed bats (12 grams) contain most energy around 140 kHz, the frequency to which its ears are mechanically tuned. Old World leaf-nosed bats and some other species can broadcast echolocation calls and receive echoes from them at the same time.

340 meters per second in air, so the echo from an insect 1 meter away returns in about 3 milliseconds (ms, or thousandths of a second), while the echo from an insect 5 meters away comes back in about 15 milliseconds. When you remember that both the bat and its target can be flying, it is obvious that bats have lightning-fast reflexes and an uncanny ability to measure time.

Signal strength is another important part of the story. The echolocation calls of a little brown bat are very strong (intense), registering about 110 decibels (dB) 10 centimeters in front of the bat. For comparison, this is stronger than the shrill howl of a smoke detector. Signal strength is important because sound loses energy as it travels through air. Some of its energy dissipates (spreads out) over distance and some is absorbed by the atmosphere (attenuates). Higher-frequency sounds, particularly ultrasonic ones, are more vulnerable to attenuation than lower-frequency sounds. This is why foghorns are bass in pitch.

For a little brown bat, the 110-decibel signal has lost over half of its energy by the time it has traveled about 10 meters, and the same processes weaken the returning echo. We can assume that bats are like humans and can hear sounds stronger than 0 decibels. If so, judging from the strength of the bat's signal and the frequencies contained therein, an echolocating little brown bat would first detect an insect-sized target at less than 5 meters. The strength of the signal, whether of the original sound or its echo, is crucial in echolocation. Bats

have specializations to enhance both the strength of their echolocation signals and the detection of weak echoes.

Bats can increase signal strength and range by using longer signals. Most echolocating bats separate pulse and echo in time, meaning that they cannot broadcast and receive at the same time. This means that longer signals deafen bats to the echoes returning from close targets. For example, a bat producing an echolocation signal that lasts 5 milliseconds will not hear the echoes from the insect that is only 1 meter away.

Horseshoe bats, Old World leaf-nosed bats, and Parnell's moustached bat use a different approach to echolocation, broadcasting on one frequency and receiving on another. These bats separate pulse and echo in frequency so they can broadcast and receive at the same time. This is possible because they have very specialized auditory systems which exploit Doppler-shifted echoes.

The *frequency* or pitch of the echolocation calls also affects the bat's perception of its world. Higher-frequency sounds have shorter wavelengths than lower-frequency sounds, providing the bat with more information about the fine details of the object it has detected. Most bats broadcast echolocation calls that are between 20 and 60 kHz, but some species use calls that are readily audible to humans (sounds below 15 kHz).

We know that bats change the design of their echolocation calls according to the task at hand. Bats change the duration of their signals. For example, an eastern red bat searching for a target produces calls that last about 10 milliseconds, but when it is closing with an insect, often a moth, the signals get shorter and shorter, until, just before contact, each signal lasts about 1 millisecond. Progressive shortening of the echolocation calls ensures that the bat will not deafen itself to the echoes resounding from a nearby insect. Through this chase, the bat also has changed the frequency design of its signal. When it is searching, the bat's calls sweep from about 40 to 30 kHz, while in the attack they cover 50 to 38 kHz. When searching for prey, the eastern red bat

Parnell's moustached bat (15 grams) is the only species of bat occurring in the New World that can broadcast echoloca- tion signals and receive echoes at the same time. This insec- tivorous species is widespread in the West Indies and in South and Central America.

This female eastern red bat (12 grams) uses broadband echolocation calls and sometimes feeds heavily on moths.

produces an echolocation pulse every 200 milliseconds, but one every 5 milliseconds in the final stages of the attack.

Today the echolocation or biosonar of bats is general knowledge. But in fact, biologists also know that not all bats can echolocate, and that some other animals, including some birds, toothed whales, and shrews, use echolocation.

Now it seems obvious that the faces of some bats reflect specializations for echolocation. One series of specializations for echolocation is associated with the production and emission of pulses of sound. In most echolocating bats, the pulses of sound are produced in the larynx or voice box. Very thin vocal cords vibrate as air passes over them, producing the sounds that are emitted through the bats' open mouth (most species) or their nostrils. The flaps of skin around the mouths of some bats, like the noseleafs on other bats, probably serve to direct the sounds away from the bat. The effect may be the same as the one you achieve by cupping your hands around your mouth to direct your voice.

Bats are specialized to receive sounds, particularly faint echoes. This is obvious because ears often dominate the faces of bats. In species such as eastern red bats that produce echolocation calls that cover several frequencies, the ears are relatively unspecialized. In others, like Noack's leaf-nosed bats, echolocation calls are dominated by a single frequency to which the ears are most sensitive. In this and other species, the bats' ears are mechanically tuned to the frequencies dominating the echolocation calls. This feature increases the sensitivity of the auditory system, particularly to faint echoes.

We know most about the echolocation behavior of bats that hunt airborne targets, usually flying insects. But what about the bats that are "gleaners," taking prey from surfaces such as the vegetation or the ground? This is common practice among bats, adopted by species of slit-faced bats, false vampire bats, plain-nosed bats, and New World leaf-nosed bats. If these bats used echolocation to detect, track, and evaluate their prey, they would face the challenge

Looking up at this Schmidt's large-eared bat (8 grams) makes it easy to see several features associated with echolocation. The noseleaf affects the pattern of radiation of sound away from the bat's face. The large ears and conspicuous tragus are part of the sound reception system. The extraordinary flexibility of the bat's neck allows it to look straight backward as it's doing in this picture. This species is insectivorous.

of detecting a hard target on a hard background. In other words, echoes from the prey would arrive at the bat's ears at virtually the same time as echoes from the surface on which it was sitting.

The echolocation calls of gleaning bats tend to be low in energy (intensity) and dominated by higher-frequency sounds, a combination of features that limit their utility over distances of more than 2 to 5 meters. The echolocation calls are also very brief, typically lasting a millisecond or less, another factor that may limit their effective range.

So it is no surprise that many gleaning bats do not appear to use echolocation to find food. Experiments with species ranging from Indian false vampire bats to fringe-lipped bats, California leaf-nosed bats, pallid bats, and brown long-eared bats (for example) have demonstrated how these gleaners depend upon other cues to detect and track their targets. Often, the clues are the scuffling sounds associated with movement. This appears typical of many species, including Egyptian slit-faced bats, whose ears are mechanically tuned to these lower-frequency sounds. Fringe-lipped bats listen to the calls of male frogs, while California leaf-nosed bats and Indian false vampire bats also may use vision to find their prey.

Most of the pteropodid bats, the fruit- and flower-visitors of Africa, southern Asia, and Australia (the Old World), do not echolocate. Their counterparts from South and Central America do echolocate. For fruit- and

flower-visiting bats, vision and a keen sense of smell are vital for finding food. In South and Central America, the fruit- and flower-feeding bats are accomplished echolocators, but we do not yet know the role that echolocation plays in their lives. The same is true for the blood-feeding vampire bats. Like the gleaning bats, their echolocation calls are short, low in energy, and high in frequency, all features that should restrict their echolocation to working at very short ranges. We still do not understand how these bats assemble a picture of their surroundings.

The advantage that echolocation offers to aerial-feeding bats is the ability to detect flying insects in situations with unpredictable lighting. Everyone knows how easy it can be to watch a fly walking across a light-colored ceiling. The fly is a dark spot moving against a light background. But as soon as the fly moves onto patterned wallpaper it appears and disappears according to the contrast between the fly and the background. The same is true when you try to follow the flight of an insect, bird, or bat at dusk. Against a light sky, the

flying animal is a dark silhouette. Against vegetation or other dark-colored objects, the flying animal is quickly lost to the observer's eye.

Many anatomical features of fossil bats that are at least 50 million years old suggest that they could echolocate. Like "modern" bats, these species had adaptations associated with the production of sounds (larynx) and the processing of their echoes (the auditory system). I think that the ancestors of bats could echolocate and that this behavior has been a key to bats' success. Other biologists do not agree, proposing that the ancestors of bats could not echolocate. Eventually we may know the "truth," but I am not holding my breath.

Two important disadvantages to echolocation are a short effective range and information leakage. We know that a big brown bat using echolocation first detects a June beetle–sized target at about 5 meters, about one second from contact for the bat flying 5 meters per second. This does not give the bat much time from detection to contact, leading biologists to propose that short effective range may be one reason that bats are so small. Quite simply, small animals may be able to survive a short effective range, while larger animals need more time to respond to objects in front of them. They would not be well served by the short ranges provided by echolocation. These arguments do not apply to toothed whales because the density of water is much higher than the density of air. This means that sounds travel about three times as fast in water as they do in air.

The strength of the echolocation signals (110 dB) of bats hunting airborne targets and the numbers of calls that they produce (from 5 to over 200 per second) combine to make echolocating bats conspicuous. This is obvious to anyone who has used a bat detector, an instrument sensitive to the frequencies of sounds used by echolocating bats. The information in the calls can be used by the bat that produced the call (echolocation), and by other bats in the area (communication).

Next to echolocation, one of the most remarkable discoveries involving bats is the fact that many insects have ears that can detect the echolocation calls of bats. Moths, mantises, lacewings, some beetles, and many crickets are examples of insects with bat detectors. The average moth first hears an approaching eastern red bat at about 40 meters, while the bat might detect this moth at 10 meters. Upon hearing a series of weak (faint) echolocation

An Egyptian slit-faced bat (10 grams) prepares to eat a grasshopper that it has caught. The ears of this gleaning bat are very sensitive to low-frequency sounds (below 5 kHz) often associated with movement. Unlike in some other bats, the tuning of its ears is not related to the sounds dominating the echolocation calls. Egyptian slit-faced bats are widespread in Africa.

A short-tailed fruit bat (16 grams) from Mexico is an accomplished echolocator, but we have little information about the role that echolocation plays in the life of this species.

calls, the moth turns and flies in the opposite direction, and probably never appears on the bat's screen. This is electronic (acoustic) warfare at its best.

But the warfare escalates. Some tiger moths have noisemakers, and they produce a series of clicks in response to the echolocation calls of a bat that is about to attack them. The moth's clicks cause some bats to abort their attacks. Three theories have been proposed to explain the bats' responses to the moths' clicks. Everyone agrees that the moths' clicks are well designed to get the attention of many echolocating bats. The simplest explanation for the bats' behavior is that the attacking bat is startled, surprised by a burst of sounds from a target. There is evidence to support this view. A more complicated theory proposes that the moth's sounds jam the bat's echolocation system, and other evidence supports this theory. A third theory notes that many tiger moths are bad tasting and proposes that the clicks of these moths are acoustic warnings about distastefulness. In other words, some tiger moths behave like monarch butterflies, advertising their bad taste. Once again, there is evidence supporting this interpretation.

Does there have to be one "right" answer? When there are at least 400 species of bats that hunt flying insects and literally hundreds of species of tiger moths, there is no reason to believe that one theory is correct and the others incorrect. We know that bats learn about the defensive behavior of their insect prey and learn to associate sounds like moth clicks with bad taste. Some work

with captive big brown bats demonstrated that a bat's response to moth clicks depends upon its prior experience. Today the mystery may be as much with the moths as it is with the bats.

Echolocation is one of the most astounding discoveries about animal behavior. From the time of Spallanzani, biologists have been fascinated by the hearing abilities of bats. As a result, too often the visual abilities of bats have been ignored in studies of their behavior. Once again, Donald Griffin has led the way. In 1967, he and some colleagues demonstrated the importance of vision to greater spear-nosed bats. The study animals had been taken from their home cave and released at different distances to assess how effectively the bats could find their way home. Through the use of blindfolds (goggles) and radio tags, Griffin and his team showed how the bats that could see were fastest at getting home. Blindfolded bats eventually got home but took longer and followed more circuitous routes than the ones with unimpaired vision.

THREE

WHAT BATS EAT

There are several remarkable things about the diets of bats: the range of food on their menus, the amounts of food they consume, and the variety of strategies they use in finding food. Ironically this diversity is only partly evident from a glance at bats' teeth.

Bats that eat animals have relatively consistent tooth design, whether the food is fish, insects, or other bats. Their molar teeth tend to be W-shaped, providing surfaces that both shear and crush food. Fruit-eating bats tend to have molars with flatter surfaces for crushing. This is evident both in the New World leaf-nosed bats and the Old World fruit bats. The flower-visiting bats have long faces and small teeth that lack crushing surfaces, whether you find them in the New World or in the Old World. The most specialized of bats, the

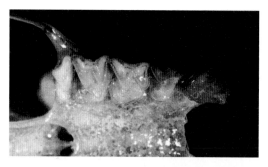

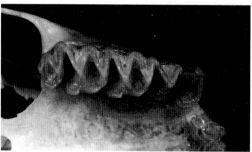

The cheek teeth (molars) of animal-eating bats share a typical W-shaped pattern. Both the yellow-winged bat from East Africa and the greater bulldog bat from the New World tropics eat animals; the former usually insects, the latter fish, fiddler crabs, and insects.

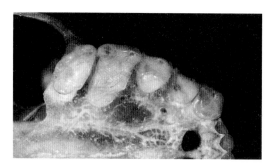

The cheek teeth of an intermediate fruit bat, a species from Central and South America, have flattened surfaces for crushing fruit.

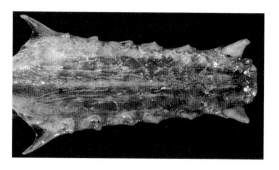

Crushing fruit also appears to be the main function of the flattened cheek teeth of a short-nosed fruit bat, a fruit-eating bat from Southeast Asia.

The elongated muzzle of this Mexican long-tongued bat bears very small teeth with virtually no crushing surfaces. This bat from the New World tropics visits flowers where it feeds on nectar and pollen.

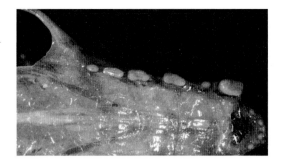

Like its New World flower-visiting counter-part, Woermann's bat has teeth with virtually no crushing surfaces. Woermann's bat lives mainly in the rain forests of Africa.

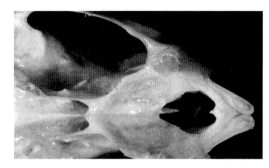

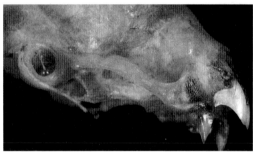

Looking straight down on the teeth of a common vampire bat makes it easy to appreciate the bladelike incisor and canine teeth. The side view presents a different perspective of these highly specialized teeth, which are razor-sharp and lack enamel.

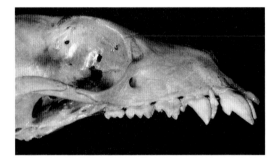

A side view of the teeth of Whitehead's fruit bat from the Philippines reveals molars with many cusps. We do not yet know whether or not these spectacular teeth are associated with specialized feeding behavior. Whitehead's fruit bats are presumed to feed mainly on fruit.

The mandibles of a beetle are embedded in the wrinkled lip of this little free-tailed bat (10 grams). This bat occurs widely in Africa, where it often roosts in bridges, buildings, and hollow trees.

blood-feeding vampires, have the most distinctive teeth of all, from the blade-like incisors and canines to the small cheek teeth that serve so well in clipping fur and feathers. Some bats, like Whitehead's fruit bat, have spectacular molars with many small cusps.

THE VARIETY OF FOOD

Bats eat an astonishing array of food. The menu includes other animals, leaves, fruit, nectar and pollen, and blood. The range of animals eaten is also impressive, from tiny insects such as midges to large dung beetles and moths, from fish to frogs, birds, and other bats. Bigger bats usually eat larger prey than smaller ones. For example, little brown bats (weighing about 8 grams) eat mainly small aquatic insects such as midges, while the larger big brown bats (16 grams) often eat June beetles. The same principle applies to bats that eat fruit and other animals.

Most bats eat insects. Northern long-eared bats, for instance, often eat underwing moths. Some insects leave painful reminders of their passing, as for example the head of a beetle attached by its mandibles to the lips of a little free-tailed bat. Insectivorous

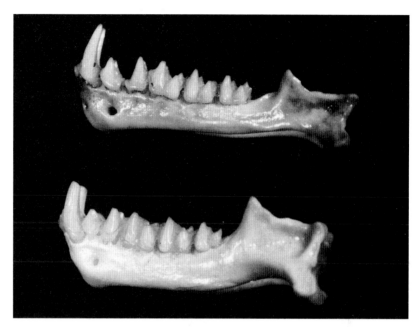

Bats that feed mainly on soft-bodied insects such as moths (Martienssen's free-tailed bat from Africa) have lighter lower jaws (top) than species that feed more on hard-bodied insects such as beetles (a common free-tailed bat from South America).

bats do not appear to specialize in any particular species of insect. Still, the basic appearances of bats' lower jaws offers us some clues about diet. Bat species with lighter jaw bones and teeth probably eat more softer-bodied insects (moths, midges) than harder-bodied insects (beetles and bugs). The bats that eat more beetles and bugs tend to have bigger jaw bones and larger teeth.

At 30 grams, this large slit-faced bat is one of the top predators along the Zambezi River. This bat eats an astonishing array of other animals, from bats to birds, fish to frogs and insects.

But bats, particularly the larger species (by bat standards this means anything over 30 grams), also eat other animals. Large slit-faced bats provide a realistic example. Along the Zambezi River in Zimbabwe these bats regularly consume large insects, fish, frogs, small birds, and even other bats. For most of the year frogs appear to be the staple

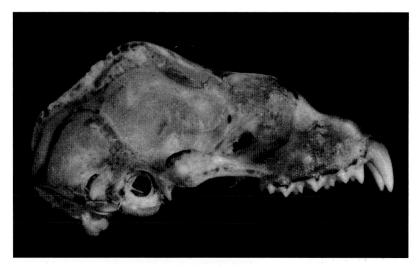

diet, but the bats take an impressive array of other food. The sight of one of these large slit-faced bats catching, killing, and then eating an Egyptian slit-faced bat (about one third its size) is not one to forget. The skull of this bat is dominated by a prominent sagittal crest, which translates into a powerful bite. Elsewhere in the world, bats like Linnaeus' false vampire bat will eat birds and other bats, while bulldog bats hunt over water and the larger species often takes fish.

Bats appear to show two kinds of fishing behavior. The bulldog bats, fishing bats, and some mouse-eared bats have enlarged hind feet with prominent claws that they use to snatch small fish from the water and fiddler crabs from the beach. In cross-section, the claws appear to be designed to minimize the cost of pulling them through the water. As far as I know, nobody has ever seen a large slit-faced bat catch a fish. These bats, like Indian false vampire bats, do

The skull of a large slit-faced bat shows a well-developed sagittal crest and strong teeth. Large slit-faced bats use a powerful bite to subdue prey such as Egyptian slit-faced bats.

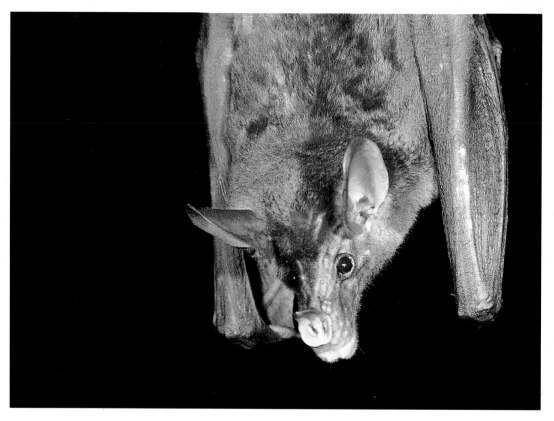

Linnaeus' false vampire bat at 150 grams occurs in South and Central America and is the largest bat of the New World. This predator is a scaled-up version of the large slit-faced bat, taking a wide range of food, including birds and other bats.

eat fish from time to time. They lack enlarged hind feet and claws and I suspect that they catch fish in their mouths. In India, Indian false vampire bats have been observed using their mouths to snatch frogs from the water's surface, as have fringe-lipped bats in Panama. We do not know of any bats that, like kingfishers and other birds, dive in pursuit of fish.

In tropical regions around the world, many species of fruit bats eat figs. In the woodlands of Africa, epauletted fruit bats are widespread, and the distinctive calls of males advertising for females are familiar sounds of the African night. These bats regularly handle up to three times their body weight in fruit (often figs) every night and disperse the seeds far and wide. In South and Central America, species of New World leaf-nosed bats comprise the fruit-

This lesser bulldog bat (30 grams) from South and Central America is one species that occasionally takes fish, but more often flying insects.

eating team. These bats, as their name implies, have leaflike structures on their noses, apparently reflecting their echolocation behavior. The fruit bats of the Old World tropics, from Africa to Australia, have the more doglike faces like that of the epauletted fruit bat. Many fruit-eating bats also eat leaves, a behavior that, until recently, was not associated with bats. New leaves provide bats with an important source of protein and sugars.

In the tropics and subtropics around the world many species of bats feed on the nectar and pollen they collect from flowers. In the Old World tropics pteropodid bats fill this role, while in South and Central America it is New World leaf-nosed bats. In both cases, elongated muzzles are prominent in these bats and are combined with long, distensible tongues. Flower bats of the New World, like the small long-faced bat, have conspicuous whiskers.

Naturally, the blood-feeding vampires are the most notorious of bats. The three species of vampires live in South and Central America, occurring from northern Mexico down into Argentina and Chile. These bats have remarkably sharp teeth. While the common vampire bat is agile on the ground and perhaps does most of its feeding there, the hairy-legged vampire is more arboreal, presumably stalking its prey among the foliage and branches of trees. The common vampire bat has elongated thumbs that serve like throwing sticks to launch the bat from the ground. The hairy-legged vampire bat has shorter thumbs but its calcars give it almost prehensile hind feet, perfect for gripping branches.

Vampire bats use chemicals to counter the antibleeding defenses of their prey. The bats' saliva contains ingredients that inhibit clotting and promote local bleeding. This and the nature of the wound combine to deliver to the hungry bat the 2 tablespoons or so of blood that it needs. Contrary to popular belief, vampire bats do not "go for the throat" or break into large blood

The figs growing on this tree make it a nightly feeding stop for epauletted fruit bats.

Epauletted fruit bats (90 grams) occur widely through the savannah woodlands of Africa and for much of the year these bats depend upon figs as their staple food. The doglike face is typical of the fruit bats of the Old World, sometimes known as "flying foxes."

vessels like veins or arteries. Instead they remove a small (5 mm diameter) divot of skin and exploit the superficial bleeding which they promote with their saliva and by the action of their tongues.

HOW MUCH BATS EAT!

There are many "facts" about just what bats eat. On average, insectivorous bats eat half their body weight in insects each night they are active. When producing milk to feed their young, female insectivorous bats eat their own body weight in insects each night. But bats also are said to eat several hundred insects in an hour. This is misleading because what a bat actually eats depends upon its size and the size of its prey. For example, the Schmidt's large-

Fruit bats in the New World like this pygmy fruit bat (10 grams) are smaller than their Old World counterparts, and most species have prominent noseleafs. Like other New World leaf-nosed bats, pygmy fruit bats are echolocators.

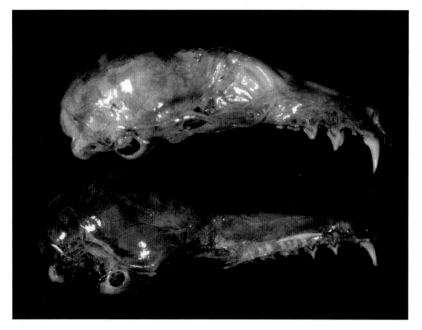

Nectar-feeding bats tend to have long faces with prominent canine (eye) teeth and smaller molars. This trend is obvious in Woermann's bat (top), an Old World nectar-feeder from Africa, and more obvious in the Mexican long-tongued bat (bottom) from the New World.

eared bat weighs about 8 grams, less than a fly that almost fills the palm of my hand. Now bats may eat a great deal, but one of these bats is unlikely to eat even one of these flies, let alone several hundred of them in an hour.

The impressive appetites of bats can be expressed as the number of mosquitoes a bat might consume in a night. A little brown bat is said to eat up to 4,000 mosquitoes a night, about half its body weight. This "fact" is used to support the argument that bats are beneficial. But how often do little brown bats eat mosquitoes, let alone 4,000 of them a night? Several years ago in August, some students working with me caught little brown bats that were visiting caves and mines. The students collected and analyzed droppings from the bats, comparing what they found to what mosquitoes looked like after they had been through a bat. Each night at each location some of the bats had eaten a few mosquitoes. Other insects (usually midges and caddis flies) dominated the diet as they have in other studies of the feeding ecology of little brown bats. The depiction of little brown bats as a scourge of mosquitoes is misleading, however much people would like to believe it. But when there are hundreds of species of insectivorous bats in the world, many of them weighing less than 10 grams as adults, I expect that some

will turn out to eat mosquitoes at least some of the time. Bodenheimer's pipistrelle, a 3- to 4-gram species from the Middle East, is a case in point. At some oases in Israel these bats often eat mosquitoes.

FINDING AND CATCHING THEIR FOOD

Animal-eating bats appear to have two basic approaches to hunting. Many species, like little brown bats that feed on flying insects, fly continuously as they hunt. These and other bats that feed on flying insects catch their prey in their wing and tail membranes. Other species, such as the large slit-faced bats, usually sit on a perch and wait for something edible to come within range. When they are first learning to fly, little brown bats also may sit and wait for a passing target, while in times when food is scarce, large slit-faced bats will fly continuously searching for something to eat.

Fruit-eating bats appear to grab their food directly in the mouth, an

This small long-faced bat (7 grams) shows the long muzzle of a nectar-feeding bat. This species is widespread in South and Central America.

A common vampire bat (35 grams) showing the details of the noseleaf and the upper incisor teeth. This is one of three blood-feeding species of bats.

The world's largest species of fly, photographed in Colombia by H. F. Howden.

approach that also is typical of some animal-eating bats. Large slit-faced bats, fringe-lipped bats, and others typically bite the victim's head and then take it away to eat elsewhere. As we have seen, some fishing bats catch their prey in their hind feet, and many of the bats that hunt flying insects catch them on the wing or tail membranes.

The diets of bats reflect a marvelous variety of morphology and behavior, demonstrating just how these mammals have evolved to fill a wide range of roles in the ecosystems where they occur.

Bodenheimer's pipistrelle is a tiny (3 gram) species that occurs in the desert areas of the Middle East. Little is known about the details of the biology of this insectivorous species.

FOUR

SURVIVING THE DAY: WHERE BATS ROOST

These epauletted fruit bats were roosting in a small tree. The flash has lighted the bats' eyes, making them more conspicuous and partly neutralizing the disruptive coloration provided by white tufts below their ears.

Most bats are very secretive about where they spend the day, their "day roosts." This is reflected by the reality that we know little about the day roosts used by many of the world's 900 or so species of bats. People often think of bats as being creatures of caves, and it is true that caves are the day roosts of some species of bats. But many (most?) of the world's bats never venture into caves at all, roosting elsewhere in a variety of places. Some bat species are very specialized in their selection of day roosts. For example, in Malaysia, two species of club-footed bats roost in the hollows of bamboo stems. In Australia and elsewhere in the world, some bats roost in abandoned birds' nests such as the domed nests of weaver-birds, orioles, or cliff swallows. In Central and South America and in Southeast Asia, several species

A Mauritian tomb bat (15 grams), an insectivorous species, roosting on the trunk of a tree in Kruger National Park in South Africa. The bat's coloration and small size combine to make it almost invisible to the casual observer. Once again, the reflection of the flash in the bat's eyes makes it more conspicuous.

build tents by biting leaves so that they fold over and envelop roosting bats.

Small size is an asset for animals that are trying to hide during the day, and it certainly works for most bats. I suspect that as we find out more about the roosting habits of bats, we will discover that many species roost among the foliage of trees and vines. Roosting Wahlberg's epauletted fruit bats illustrate a typical foliage roost. By remaining relatively still and quiet, the bats are easy to overlook among the tangle of leaves and branches. Furthermore, the white spots at the bases of their ears probably serve as "disruptive coloration," breaking up the outline of the bat's silhouette against the dappled background of the sun coming through the canopy.

At a body weight of about 90 grams, the Wahlberg's epauletted fruit bats are more than three times bigger than hoary bats and more than eight times bigger than eastern red bats, two American species that also roost among foliage. Between 1988 and 1993 at Pinery Provincial Park in southwestern Ontario, we used radio tracking to

A group of ten proboscis bats (4 grams) roost in a line on the underside of a tree branch overhanging a stream in Costa Rica. The dark color of the bats contrasts sharply with the light-colored tree branch. This insectivorous species is widespread in South and Central America. **Photograph by Jenna Dunlop.**

Two Peters bats (6 grams) roost on the side of a breezeway on a building in Costa Rica. We had banded one of the bats so that we could follow its choice of roosts over time. These bats are alert and quick to take flight if disturbed. This insectivorous species occurs in Central and South America.

study the behavior of eastern red and hoary bats. Although we could easily locate the specific oak tree in which radio-tagged individuals roosted, we never spotted a roosting bat. The combination of the bats' small size, distracting leaves and branches, coloration, and lighting presumably all contributed to this reality.

Other bats are more brazen in their selection of roosts, often sitting in the open on surfaces such as the trunks of trees. Clearly the contrast between the

bat and its background is a key to its conspicuousness. For example, the Mauritian tomb bat is difficult to spot on the trunk of a tree, while the proboscis bats stand out sharply against the light-colored tree trunks they like to use as a day roost.

Proboscis bats and Mauritian tomb bats are sheath-tailed bats, which often roost on horizontal surfaces. These bats are usually very alert and active in their roosts, quickly taking flight and moving elsewhere if disturbed or

A portrait of a Peters bat shows clearly that the eyes are large and conspicuous and the ears have pleats which allow it to fold back its ears.

A little brown bat emerging from a tree hollow via the workings of a pileated woodpecker.

closely approached. The typical posture of a roosting sheath-tailed bat is obvious in the picture on p. 62, showing Peters bats roosting on the side of a building. The bats roost head-down, bracing their wrists against the roost surface and arching their necks and backs so that they can look straight out. Sheath-tailed bats, like Peters bats, are large-eyed and gentle. Most are relatively small (the Peters bat weighs about 6 grams, the proboscis bat about 4 grams, and the Mauritian tomb bat about 20 grams). The stain on the wall where the Peters bats are roosting is more than just an accumulation of urine and droppings. Sheath-tailed bats, like many other species, have special glands that produce secretions that function in communication, marking the roosting site of an

In 1997 this bat house, located on the side of an ash tree in the suburbs of Toronto, had been up for seven years. No bats had occupied it. The house is 0.7 metres high.

individual and probably conveying information about its condition.

Many bats prefer to roost in more sheltered situations, such as the space under loose bark on the trunk of a tree, or within hollows in trees. Sheltered roosts typically provide some protection from the elements, and by selecting locations that face south and west, bats also may benefit from solar heating in the afternoon. Hollows, which are more common in older than in younger trees, can be vital to bats that must rely on existing openings to gain access to these roosts. For example, a colony of ten to twenty big brown bats regularly roosted in a hollow tree in south-central British Columbia. Bats that roost in

Little brown bats in one of the bat houses at Nipigon. The screen lining the bat houses gives them purchase and makes it easier for them to move around in the house.

hollow trees typically change roosts almost every day, moving from hollow to hollow. The roost-switching behavior became obvious only when biologists were able to radio-track (see next chapter) the bats. It remains unclear just why bats would switch roosts this way, but there are several possible explanations. The bats may be avoiding predators that learn where they roost and try to ambush them as they leave. Alternatively, the bats might move to avoid accumulations of parasites such as fleas and bedbugs. They also might move to different roosts according to local conditions of temperature or food availability. More than one of these explanations may apply in many situations and for different bats.

Two little brown bats hibernate in an abandoned mine in southern Ontario. Note the droplets of water (condensation) that bedeck the fur and whiskers of the bats.

In eastern North America, big brown bats often spend their summer days inside buildings. The bats typically choose warm places such as those in attics or under the eaves. Radio-tracking studies of big brown bats in Ontario and other places in eastern North America have revealed that these bats are extremely roost-faithful, returning day after day, year after year to the same building sites. This contrasts with the behavior of big brown bats roosting in trees in British Columbia. In buildings, bats often come in conflict with people who would prefer them to roost elsewhere.

Roosting bats leave accumulations of guano, their droppings. Large num-

In January, stalagmites of ice grow up from the floor of the entrance chamber in a cave in southern Ontario. Above, bats hibernate in nooks and crannies on the ceiling, in areas where the temperatures are just above freezing.

bers of bats produce more guano, so that the level of odor associated with roosting bats usually is a function of the size of the colony and the time that the bats have used the roost. In extreme situations, "pissicles," stalactitelike structures composed of crystallized bat urine and bat feces, festoon the roof supports in attics that harbor large numbers of bats.

It is relatively easy to encourage bats to move to another roost site. Repeated disturbances usually cause them to move. Once the bats have departed, the entrances they have used can be sealed with lightweight building materials such as caulking and screening. The teeth and claws of bats are not strong enough to allow them to make their own openings to gain access to buildings, which makes the job easier. But what happens to the bats that are evicted from their roosts?

For bats that change roosts often, eviction appears to present no particular difficulty. For example, in Ontario, big brown bats evicted from one building simply move next door. Others, such as little brown bats at Chautauqua, New York, just disappear. Since bats continue to find and exploit new roosting opportunities, their patterns of behavior must include some mechanisms for the exploration and assessment of potential roosts. There are many examples of bats moving into new buildings, but we do not yet understand just how they find and evaluate new sites.

So what can a homeowner with bats do if evicting them is the obvious option, but there is also concern about protecting bats and not wanting to harm them? Bat houses, also known as bat boxes, could offer an alternative. Bat houses, similar to bird houses, are designed to accommodate roosting bats. In parts of the United Kingdom, massive volunteer efforts have resulted in the placement of literally thousands of bat houses in some wooded areas. Approximately 5 percent of the houses have been occupied by bats, giving biologists ideally accessible study populations of bats. Elsewhere, bat houses have been less successful.

In spite of repeated efforts in a variety of areas in the United States and Canada, many bat houses remain unoccupied by bats. Still, every summer nature and garden centers sell hundreds of bat houses as people strive to be more bat-friendly. My own experience with bat houses has been disappointing. At the Chautauqua Institution in New York, over six years, some of my students installed over 100 bat houses. None attracted bats, even though we estimated that there were 10,000 little brown bats living in buildings on the Institution's ground. At my home in Toronto a noble bat house has remained unoccupied over seven years, even though big brown bats regularly pass within a few meters of it on their nightly comings and goings.

My experience left me with the impression that bat houses did not successfully attract bats. Meanwhile, reports from near Nipigon, Ontario, indicated that each summer large numbers of bats appeared and spent a few days around a Trans Canada Pipelines compressor and power station. The bats arrived after the weather had warmed up slightly, but stayed only a few days. While they were in the area, one could find roosting bats "everywhere," from the nooks and crannies around buildings to the spaces between signs affixed to chain-link fences.

These roosting bats attracted some attention from local naturalists and even more from the local ravens, which quickly learned to look for, extract, and eat the roosting bats. We installed some bat houses in the area and a few migrating bats took advantage of them. While none of the bats established a nursery colony in the bat houses at Nipigon, the migrating animals, mainly little brown bats, often used them for a night or two as they moved through the area.

Sparks fly as a welder builds a gate across the entrance of an abandoned mine that harbors hundreds of hibernating bats each winter.

Do bat houses work? The answer could be "yes" or "no," depending upon the bats, the local conditions, and, perhaps, the structure of the bat house. How do bats find bat houses? If we knew the answer to that question, it might be much easier to make these structures work as tools for bat conservation.

In winter, the scene changes dramatically for bats in the temperate regions of the world. Some migrate to warmer areas where winters are less severe and they can remain active. For others, hibernation is the main strategy for over-wintering. Some species make lengthy migrations between summer roosts and hibernation sites. During hibernation, the bat is "out cold" or torpid as its body temperature drops to that of its surroundings. In southern Ontario this is between 0° and 5° C for bats hibernating in caves or mines. Some bats, like little browns, also require very high levels of humidity in their hibernation sites. Meanwhile, species such as big brown bats and eastern small-footed bats tolerate drier conditions.

The climate within a cave during the winter can vary. While the floor may be regularly below freezing, the ceiling can offer bats the above-freezing conditions that they require. The energy available to a hibernating bat is just the fat on its body, in autumn about 25 percent of its body mass. The most expensive part of hibernation is arousal, times when the bats wake up and become active.

In parts of the world where bats hibernate in caves and mines, disturbance during the hibernation season can be fatal. One extraordinary thing about hibernating bats is that even though they are out cold, they remain very aware of their surroundings. Disturbances, such as people walking by or closely approaching hibernating bats, cause them to arouse, and within twenty minutes they can be ready to take flight. A single arousal can cost a little brown bat the energy stores that would have allowed it to hibernate for over sixty days.

To protect hibernating bats, conservationists frequently build gates across the entrances to caves and mines that serve as hibernation sites. In places where old mine workings pose a hazard to people, the gates serve a dual function, protecting both people and bats. While it is true that flying bats must slow down to negotiate the gates, in turn making them more vulnerable to predators, gates have translated into the survival of many bats.

Roosts have always been vital for bats, a reality that helps us to understand their secrecy on this topic. Finding a bat's roost(s) is easiest when you have a radio transmitter on the bat. The study of bat roosts will no doubt continue to intrigue biologists for many years to come.

FIVE

THE APPEARANCE OF BATS

Hemprich's big-eared bat (22 grams) is a spectacular insectivorous species that occurs from North Africa to China. It is a species of arid and semiarid areas.

The appearance of bats provide biologists with important indications about their behavior and performance. Wings and ears offer two excellent examples. The overall shape and size of a bat's wings, like those of an aeroplane, allow us to predict flight performance. Some bats have long and narrow wings, usually associated with rapid, low-cost, and relatively unmaneuverable flight. Others have shorter and broader wings, typical of species that are more maneuverable and fly more slowly. The importance of sounds in the lives of bats makes ears obvious points of interest for biologists interested in the lifestyles of these animals. First, let's consider wings.

Red mastiff bats have short, sleek fur which minimizes the costs of drag during flight. Their long and narrow wings translate into reduced costs of flight.

THE RED MASTIFF BAT

This medium-sized (30 grams) species of free-tailed bat is widespread in South and Central America, where it frequently roosts in buildings. Like most other free-tailed bats, red mastiff bats have long, narrow, and pointed wings and are thought to fly high and fast in pursuit of insect prey. Free-tailed bats often live in large colonies, the most spectacular being the literally millions of Mexican free-tailed bats living in some caves in the southwestern United States. To date, nobody has reported such large colonies of red mastiff bats. In spite of their

The group that studied red mastiff bats in Akumal, Mexico, in January 1996. From the right, Bill Scully (York), Burton Lim (Royal Ontario Museum), Elissa Odgren (York), Brock Fenton, Mark Hovorka (York), Christine Portfors (York), Jorge Ortega (Universidad Nacional Autonomea de México, UNAM), Sylvie Bouchard (York), Naas Rautenbach (Transvaal Museum), Jens Rydell (University of Gotenburg), Daphne Syme (York), Maarten Vonhof (York). Hector Arita (UNAM) is missing from the photograph.

large populations and common association with humans, we know relatively little about the foraging ecology of most free-tailed bats, and red mastiff bats are no exception.

In January 1996, a group studied red mastiff bats around Akumal in the Yucatán Peninsula of Mexico. We wanted to find out just how much time red mastiff bats spent foraging and what insects they ate. At Akumal, a colony of about thirty red mastiff bats roosted by day in the cinderblock wall of a house.

We planned to use radio telemetry to monitor the movements of the bats, which meant catching them and attaching radio transmitters to them. These miniature radios emit signals that can be detected with an appropriate receiver. Radio transmitters have opened up a new world for those who study bats and other animals. First used on bats in the mid-1960s to study the homing abilities of greater spear-nosed bats, radio transmitters allow biologists to monitor the behavior of marked animals. This can mean finding where the animals

The very small radio transmitter, the white structure on the blue stripe, designed for use on bats, is dwarfed atop the radio tag designed for elephants.

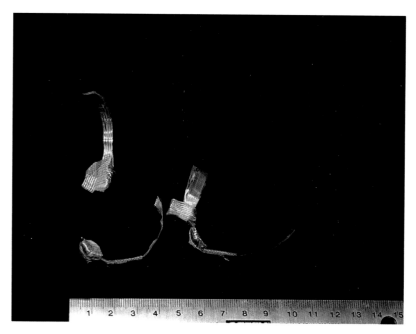

These used radio tags were removed from red mastiff bats at the end of our study in Akumal. The collars are made of fiber tape and the antennae are missing from the transmitters, presumably because the bats had bitten them off.

roost, when they emerge each night, and when they return.

But putting a tag on an animal presents several problems. Tags that are too large interfere with an animal's behavior or make it more vulnerable to its predators. To be effective, tags must be attached in a way that minimizes the impact on the animals. We know that radio tags weighing more than 5 percent of a bat's body mass interfere with the animal's maneuverability and increase its costs of flight. Working with larger animals gives biologists more latitude in their choice of tags. We made tiny collars of fiber tape to attach the transmitters to the bats. The entire package, collar and tag, weighed about 0.8 grams, or 3 percent of each bat's body mass.

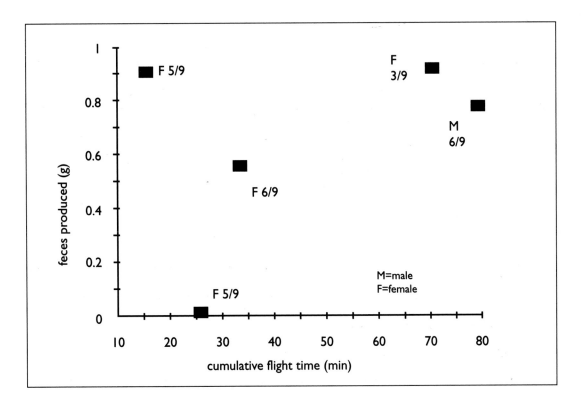

This graph shows the behavior of four female and one male red mastiff bats (solid squares) during a January 1996 study in Akumal, Mexico. Each bat spent different amounts of time flying and, upon their return to the roost, each produced different amounts of feces, reflecting the insects they had caught during their flights. One bat came home empty, but each of the others was much more successful. The numbers beside each symbol (e.g., 5/9) indicate that on five of nine nights the bats went out to forage; the other nights they stayed home.

Kuhl's pipistrelle (6 grams) is an insectivorous species occurring from southern Europe through much of Africa.

We caught the bats by netting them as they left the roost. For each bat, we measured and recorded body mass, wing shape, and area as well as forearm length. We then attached radio collars to six of them, released the tagged bats into the roost, and sat back to wait. Sunset that evening found us waiting at different locations around Akumal. We subdivided ourselves into four groups, each with a receiver and a walkie-talkie, and eagerly awaited the bats' emergence. On the first night, none of the bats with radio tags left the roost. Nor did any of them emerge on the second night.

By now I was worried that our improvised radio collars had fallen off of

the bats and that we were studying the behavior of radio collars lying in a hollow wall. But the weather had been unusually cool as a *norte* prevailed in the area, and on the third night all of the radio-tagged bats left the roost and quickly flew out of range.

For the next ten days we monitored the comings and goings of the radio-tagged red mastiff bats. On many nights the radio-tagged bats did not emerge at all, and on nights when they did, they sometimes were out for less than one hour. On the last night of our study, we monitored the bats' departures and caught five of the six as they returned. For these bats we knew exactly how

The trident leaf-nosed bat (15 grams) occurs widely in North Africa. This insectivorous species belongs to the Hipposideridae, the Old World leaf-nosed bats.

The western big-
eared bat (10 grams),
an insectivorous
species from the
western United
States and Canada.
Photograph by
Maarten Vonhof.

much time they had spent foraging and, by holding the captured bats for an
hour, we obtained feces from them. This allowed us to determine not only
how much they had eaten but also which insects they had eaten.

The red mastiff bats we radio-tagged typically spent less than one hour foraging on any night. On the last night of our study, four of the five that we captured had eaten enough insects to last them for two or three days (explaining those days when the tagged bats had not emerged at all). On the last night, one radio-tagged female had caught over 3 grams of insects in twenty minutes. The gist of this is clear from the graphical presentation of the data on p. 79. The bats ate many beetles as well as a variety of other insects.

None of the bats we tagged was reproductively active, and so their costs of operation may have been low compared to other times of the year. Nevertheless, we found that red mastiff bats are efficient foragers and that the local densities of insects allow them to spend relatively little time flying. These bats do not appear to be limited by the availability of their insect prey.

Long, narrow wings mean lower flight costs and no doubt contribute to the efficiency of red mastiff bats. In a future study we will return to Akumal when the bats have their young to get an indication of how their behavior changes when their costs of operation are higher. At that time, the bats should spend more time foraging and less time in the roost.

THE EARS HAVE IT

It is not surprising that ears should dominate the faces of microchiropteran bats because of the pervasive role that hearing plays in their lives. And yet, there is more to the story of bats' ears than first meets the eye. The variations

Big-eared brown bats (12 grams) occur widely in South America but have been little studied. This insectivorous species hunts flying insects, including fireflies. Photograph by Bill Scully.

reflect the fact that different sounds are important to bats in different ways.

Like Kuhl's pipistrelle, most species of bats that use echolocation to detect, track, and evaluate flying insects as prey have prominent but not spectacular ears. Kuhl's pipistrelles, which often can be seen hunting insects around lights in different parts of Europe and Africa, produce echolocation calls dominated by sounds between 30 and 26 kHz. Their ears are not sharply tuned to these frequencies like the ears of bats whose echolocation calls are dominated by one frequency, about 117 kHz for trident leaf-nosed bats. The ears of Bodenheimer's pipistrelles, which use echolocation calls dominated by sounds between 71 and 17 kHz, are similarly unspectacular.

But for their size, these pipistrelles have huge ears compared to our own. Still, they pale in comparison to bats with really big ears. Western big-eared bats have enormous ears that dominate their heads and faces. In this species,

The gray long-eared bat (10 grams), an insectivorous species that occurs through much of Europe.

The little big-eared bat (7 grams), a New World leaf-nosed bat that is widespread in South and Central America. This insectivorous species is a gleaner.

the ears are very sensitive to sounds much lower in frequency than those dominating the echolocation calls. Like large slit-faced bats, western big-eared bats have ears that give them a real advantage when it comes to hearing the scuffling sounds of movement. The same appears to be true of Hemprich's big-eared bat, a species that occurs in desert areas from North Africa across to China.

Western big-eared bats, large slit-faced bats, and Hemprich's big-eared bats appear to be "gleaners," predators that snatch prey, usually insects, from surfaces. We know that large slit-faced bats often take prey from the ground, while other species of big-eared bats, such as brown long-eared bats, take their prey from the vegetation. In July 1997 in Israel, I watched a Hemprich's big-eared bat as it flew low over the ground, occasionally dipping down to the ground apparently to attack prey.

Observations such as these are used by some biologists to equate big ears in bats with gleaning behavior. But we know of two spectacular exceptions. Big-eared brown bats, a species that is widespread in some parts of South America, have large, spectacular ears. Wagner Pedro, a colleague from Brazil, has watched these bats feeding in and around São Paulo in southern Brazil. Although big-eared brown bats may fly close to the ground on occasion, they hunt flying insects, often attacking fireflies. At a field station southeast of São Paulo, these bats ate a variety of insects, including many moths. Big-eared

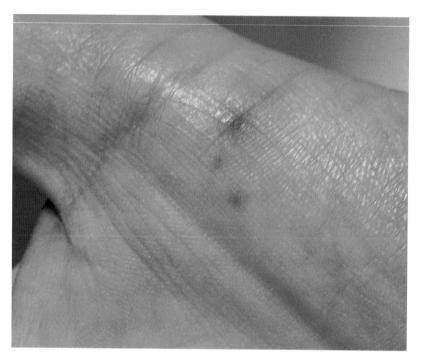

The puncture wounds resulting from the defensive bite of a 35-gram Jamaican fruit bat.

brown bats produce echolocation calls with most energy between 25 and 15 kHz, and the evidence strongly suggests that they behave like other aerial feeders and do not glean. The same is true of the spectacular spotted bat from western North America.

In short, although the appearances of bats can give us some clues about their behavior, not all bats with big ears (for example) forage in the same way. Folds or pleats are another feature of the ears of some species of bats. These can be conspicuous, and I believe that their main function is to allow the bat to fold its ear out of harm's way. This means that big-eared bats lacking the pleats will not be able to fold back their ears. One possible source of damage to a bat's ears is bites by other bats, and conspicuous ear pleats are evident in a wide range of species.

Many questions remain to be answered about the ears of bats. For example, the tragus is conspicuous in the ears of some bats such as Kuhl's pipistrelles, western big-eared bats, Hemprich's big-eared bats, gray long-eared bats, and big-eared brown bats. But not all bats have tragi (for example the trident leaf-nosed bat), and in some the tragus may be very small and inconspicuous (the little big-eared bat). What role does the tragus play? There is some evidence that in big brown bats it assists in localizing a target in vertical space, but we remain quite ignorant about its role in the biosonar of bats.

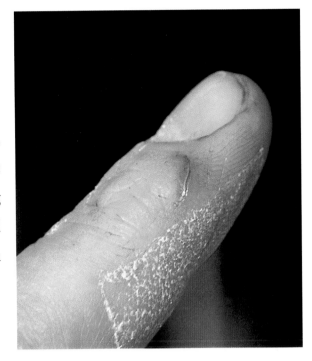

The cut resulting from the defensive bite of a 35-gram common vampire bat.

BATS AND MOTHS

Insects such as moths, mantises, beetles, and lacewings frequently have ears that allow them to hear the echolocation calls of bats. Moths hear best between 20 and 60 kHz, the frequencies most commonly used by echolocating bats. Upon hearing the echolocation calls of a bat, a moth may turn and fly away or dive for the ground. The moth appears to adjust its defensive behavior according to the strength of the bat's echolocation calls. A loud call denotes a close bat, causing the moth to dive. A faint call means a distant bat so the moth just turns and flies away from the sound source. The echolocation calls of both big-eared brown bats and spotted bats are relatively inaudible to moths (because they are strongest below 20 kHz), so that the moths would not hear the calls of these bats until the last second. In theory this means that both big-eared brown bats and spotted bats are well designed to thwart the hearing-based defenses of moths. Both of these species often eat moths, supporting the

Screwworm larvae living in a wound on the neck of a calf in Costa Rica.

theoretical predictions. The same appears to be true of other species of insectivorous bats that hunt airborne prey and use echolocation signals with most energy below 20 kHz. The European free-tailed bat, a species of southern Europe and northern Africa, is a good example of a species whose low-frequency echolocation calls make it relatively inaudible to most moths and which preys heavily on these insects.

BLOOD-FEEDING BATS

Teeth can make a difference to bats. Perhaps the "best" example, vampires, the bats that feed on blood, fire the imagination and have brought bats a good deal of notoriety. Although we tend to be repelled by thoughts of blood-feeding animals, vampire bats do offer some positive stories. For example, the prospect that the saliva of vampire bats would yield new chemicals for treating some blood diseases has presented these bats in a more wholesome light. Animals that feed on blood must counter the antibleeding defenses of their prey and develop a means of getting to the blood. While mosquitoes and many biting flies drill a tiny hole to accomplish this, the vampire bats make a larger opening.

Vampire bats have solved both of these problems. They bite to make a wound at which they can feed. The bites of bats are usually puncture wounds made by the cone-shaped canine teeth. The hole is the same that one gets from a nail. The bladelike teeth of vampire bats, however, leave a wound that looks more like a cut from a sharp knife. Other bats have canine teeth that are designed to pierce and hold food. A vampire bat's canine teeth are bladelike, but it is the upper incisor teeth that are used to make the feeding wounds. Using its upper incisor teeth, a vampire bat makes a feeding wound that is about 5 millimeters in diameter and 5 millimeters deep. Quite simply, the bat removes a divot of skin and produces a wound that will bleed freely.

A roosting yellow-shouldered bat (16 grams), a fruit-eating bat from South and Central America. With one eye the bat is watching the photographer. The leaf on the nose identifies it as a New World leaf-nosed bat.

The same yellow-shouldered bat approaches food and reveals its conspicuous shoulder gland marked by colored fur.

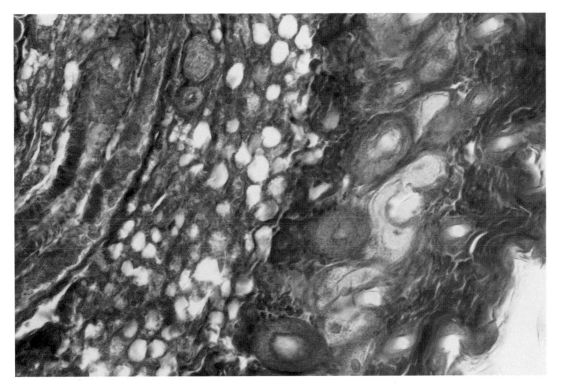

A histological section through the shoulder reveals the sebaceous glands that produce a spicy-smelling secretion. In the upper part of the photograph, hairs show as small yellow circles. The white regions beside the hairs are sebaceous glands. The cells in these glands have numerous nuclei. The blue areas are connective tissue. Fat shows as the cells with large spaces known as vacuoles. Photo by Bill Scully.

The bleeding action is promoted by the action of the bat's tongue and the chemicals in its saliva.

How did bats come to feed on blood? Are vampire bats really that different from other bats?

We know from their overall biology and structure that the three species of vampire bats (common vampire bats, white-winged vampire bats, and hairy-legged vampire bats) are closely related to the New World leaf-nosed bats, the Phyllostomidae. Their specializations for blood-feeding, which include their

A long-tailed serotine (15 grams) from southern Africa. This insectivorous species closely resembles big brown bats of North America.

teeth, saliva, and digestive systems, set the vampires apart from other New World leaf-nosed bats. Studies of their proteins suggest that vampire bats evolved more than 10 million years ago. The fossil record provides us with a relatively recent picture of vampire bats. In the last few thousand years there were other species of vampire bats, including one that was about one third larger than the living species (weighing 40 to 50 grams). Furthermore, in the recent past vampire bats occurred in Cuba and Florida and as far north as

Cape serotines (5 grams), although much smaller in body size, also resemble other bats in the genus Eptesicus, such as big brown bats.

northern California and Washington, D.C. But the fossil record sheds no light on the evolutionary origin of vampire bats.

I think that the combination of wounds on larger mammals and behavioral flexibility of the bats provides one explanation of how the ancestors of vampire bats came to feed on blood. Wounds are important in this story because they attract insects, some of which lay their eggs there. Spectacular examples of this insect behavior are provided by different species of screw-

worms. The adult female flies lay their eggs at wound sites. The eggs hatch and the larvae (maggots) move into the wound and feed there. This can make wounds important feeding sites for other animals. In Africa, two species of oxpeckers, birds related to starlings, feed at wounds and on animals (ectoparasites) such as ticks which they remove from large mammals such as giraffes, elephants, and antelope. The same feeding opportunity could have prevailed at the time before the ancestors of vampire bats began to feed on blood.

The feeding opportunity presented by wounds would be exploitable only by gleaning bats, species that look for their prey on surfaces. Fossils suggest that a gleaning lifestyle was typical of the earliest species of New World leaf-nosed bats. This evidence, and studies of the evolutionary relationships between bats in this family, indicates that species feeding on fruit, nectar and pollen, and blood are more recent developments.

While the combination of wounds and gleaning bats could explain the evolution of blood-feeding, these circumstances also prevailed in the tropics of Africa, Southeast Asia, and Australia, where bats did not adopt a blood-feeding habit. In Africa and Southeast Asia, slit-faced bats are gleaners that could have moved into a blood-feeding role. From Africa to Australia, false vampire bats also are gleaners, taking a range of prey. I believe that differences in incisor teeth explain the presence of blood-feeding bats in the New World and not in the Old World. Sharp, strong upper incisor teeth would have been essential for feeding at wounds, and the New World leaf-nosed bats are well equipped with them. Slit-faced bats, however, have tiny upper incisor teeth and false vampire bats lack them completely.

My theory about the origin of blood-feeding in bats is just that—a theory. Now we wait to see who comes up with a better one.

COMMUNICATING: ESSENCE OF BAT

A roosting bat goes unnoticed because of its small size and quiet behavior, exemplified by a yellow-shouldered bat. Enveloped by its wings, the bat is easy to overlook. The bat's dark brown shoulder patches are conspicuous when it approaches food. These patches are prominent in some male yellow-shouldered bats, but not in females. Males with conspicuous patches tend to be sexually mature, while males lacking the patches are immature.

Smoky bats (4 grams) are distinctive because of their small, clawless thumbs. This insectivorous species roosts in hollows including trees, logs, and caves and occurs widely in South America. Photograph by Maarten Vonhof.

Funnel-eared bats (6 grams), insectivorous species of the West Indies, South and Central America, often roost in caves. Little is known of their behavior. Photograph by Maarten Vonhof.

The conspicuous patch of hair marks the location of shoulder glands which give off a characteristic "spicy" odor. The hairs associated with the gland are more strawlike in texture than the body hairs, so they feel different from body hairs. A histological section of the area on the shoulder beneath the gland reveals a concentration of sebaceous glands which produce the pleasant-smelling spicy odor. The hairs associated with the gland are themselves specialized to disperse the glandular products. The specialized hairs work like paintbrushes, holding and dispersing the glands' products.

The fact that the glands are prominent only in sexually mature males suggests that they play some role in the sexual behavior of these bats. This also suggests that the glands are under hormonal control. To date we remain ignorant of the details, but in other mammals glandular secretions produced by glands like those in the shoulders of yellow-shouldered bats are used to mark other individuals (usually females) or nest/roost sites.

Scent is one medium that bats use in communication; they also depend upon both visual and acoustic signals. The shoulder area of the yellow-shouldered bat is conspicuous visually because of the contrast in color between the gland and the surrounding area. Other species of bats show similar contrasting markings that can serve in signaling.

Bats also depend upon vocalizations for communication. The signals that one individual uses in echolocation also serve in communication. The echolocation signals of aerial-feeding bats are intense and well suited to provide detailed information over some distance. Little brown bats and big brown bats that roost together produce colony-specific echolocation calls that may serve as badges of recognition.

PREDICTING THE BEHAVIOR OF BATS

Increased knowledge about specific bats makes it easier for us to predict the behavior and ecology of others. This is easiest when we are dealing with bats that are widespread and have many close relatives. We know, for example, that big brown bats of the United States and Canada hunt flying insects ranging from beetles to caddis flies, apparently reflecting the abundance of insects in areas where they are feeding. Big brown bats spend their days in buildings, hollow trees, or rock crevices, depending upon whether the bats are studied in Ontario or in British Columbia. These generalizations about foraging, diet, and roosts also apply to serotines, a species of Europe that also is in the genus *Eptesicus*. Elsewhere in the world, other species in this genus are long-tailed serotines or Cape serotines of southern Africa. Both species generally resemble big brown bats and serotines. There is, however, a drastic difference in body size between these bats, with Cape serotines weighing about 5 grams and the others between 15 and 20 grams. Future field studies can test the predictions of consistency in behavior and ecology across the genus *Eptesicus.*

It is more difficult to predict the behavior and ecology of bats that are not closely related to species that have been well studied. While we know that thumbless bats roost in caves and hollow trees, we know little else about these tiny bats (4 grams body weight). Very small thumbs that lack claws give thumbless bats their names, and two species are widespread in South and Central America. Some observations suggest that these bats hunt flying insects. In southern Brazil in 1997, we discovered that their echolocation calls are very short (less than 1 millisecond long) and high in frequency (150 to 120 kHz). If these bats do hunt flying insects, it is no surprise that they are effective predators of moths, which could not hear their echolocation calls.

In a general sense, funnel-eared bats may be relatively closely related to thumbless bats. This family (Natalidae) includes four species that occur widely in South and Central America and on some of the islands in the West Indies. Funnel-eared bats are commonly found roosting in caves, where they may form large colonies. Their small size has meant that they have received little attention from biologists studying bat behavior and ecology, and the lack of close relatives makes it difficult for us to predict more about the biology of these intriguing animals.

The appearance and behavior of bats may allow us to predict a great deal about their lifestyles and ecology. It is the exceptions that make the story interesting. Spotted bats or big-eared brown bats are excellent examples.

SIX

THE CONSERVATION OF BATS

For many years now our species, human beings, has dominated many aspects of life on planet Earth. We have held the power of life and death over other organisms so that some species which we "like" have achieved huge populations, while others that we consider to be dangerous or unpleasant have been driven to or across the brink of extinction. The examples are legion, from cattle, sheep, and other agriculturally important organisms that are beneficial to us, to wolves and other predators that have been exterminated from much of their former range. Ironically, many organisms that we have exploited to our benefit also have been driven to extinction. There are many examples, from Steller's sea cows and dodos, which are extinct, to the several species of rhinoceroses that hover at the edge of survival.

PUBLIC IMAGE

In some human cultures, bats are positive symbols. For example, in Chinese art bats are commonly presented with other symbols of good luck and long life. In the picture above, the bats appear with a tiger, with blossoms, and with fruits. The picture tells another tale as well. Small size makes bats inconspicuous and easy to overlook in the picture and in real

OPPOSITE PAGE: The details of a Mandarin square dating from between 1800 and 1830. The square is black, multicolored with blue satin, the embroidery done in the Peking knot. The tiger faces right on a mound surrounded by other Buddhist symbols, namely peaches, peonies growing from rocks, and bats. Mandarin squares were badges of rank that were worn on robes.

A yawning pygmy fruit bat.

Silver-haired bats (12 grams) like this one occur widely in the United States and Canada. These insectivorous bats form colonies in trees, under loose slabs of bark or in hollows. Populations in Canada and the northern United States migrate south for the winter.

life. Typically, bats have not suffered directly at the hands of humans.

Of course there are exceptions. Some human societies consider large fruit bats to be festive food, and human hunting pressure threatens the survival of some of these species. This is particularly true on some of the isolated islands in the South Pacific, where the introduction of firearms made it possible for human hunters to harvest more flying foxes. This change in hunting practice meant that a traditional hunt that apparently had not had too adverse an effect on the flying fox population now had a fatal impact. In the past, when hunters harvested the bats by catching them in nooses on the ends of long poles, the bats could reproduce faster than the humans could harvest them. The later use of shotguns changed the balance.

For most bat species in the world, however, their small size means that they have not been the target of human hunting pressure. Quite simply, bat ivory (their teeth), bat fur, and bat meat come in such small packages that they have not been worth exploiting.

Although bats may find the subject boring, image has a great deal to do with conservation and conservation efforts. An example is the panda logo known far and wide as the symbol of the World Wildlife Fund. Where bats are viewed as dangerous animals or as symbols of evil, there has been little public sympathy for them. Furthermore, our general ignorance about these animals has made it easy to fear them. The association

California myotis are widespread in the western United States and Canada, where they often inhabit forested areas. At adult body weights of about 5 grams, these bats appear to have smaller home ranges than the larger species that occur in the same habitat.

of bats with rabies does little to foster a positive public image for them.

All mammals are susceptible to rabies, a disease caused by a virus and usually spread by the bites of an infected animal. Bats are no exception, but they often are considered to be "carriers" of rabies, implying that they are not affected by it. In fact bats are not carriers of rabies because the disease kills them.

The strains of rabies that appear in bats differ from those that prevail in other mammals such as foxes, raccoons, and jackals. One strain of rabies is known from silver-haired bats, a tree-dwelling species of the United States and Canada. Alarmingly, in Canada and the United States, several recent human deaths from rabies have involved the silver-haired bat strain of the virus. To be specific, there were 22 human deaths from rabies in the United States between 1990 and 1996. Five of these arose from rabies contracted abroad; 15 of the remaining 17 cases involved rabies from bats, 10 the silver-haired bat strain. Fortunately, silver-haired bats do not usually roost in buildings and rarely come in contact with humans.

Like most other mammals, bats will bite in self-defence. Although they are small (silver-haired bats weigh about 12 grams as adults), a biting bat can break the skin. This reality, coupled with the occasional occurrence of rabies in bats, is good reason for people to avoid handling bats. Sensible biologists who work with bats get preexposure immunization against rabies and follow this up with booster shots if they are exposed to known rabid animals.

One other factor compounds the public health image of bats. In some parts of the world, usually the tropics and subtropics, the droppings of bats are associated with histoplasmosis, a fungus disease that affects the lungs. Like many other human afflictions, histoplasmosis often has little negative impact on individuals that contract it, but in some cases it can be serious and even fatal. Sensible people who work in bat colonies where there are accumulations of guano (droppings) wear masks that filter out particles larger than 2

microns in diameter, a step that protects them from histoplasmosis.

The negative image generated by bats' perceived involvement with diseases that affect humans is used to identify them as dangerous and harmful creatures. This portrayal can be used to justify vandalism directed at bats, and this has included wanton killing of them.

HABITAT PRESERVATION

Habitat destruction is a major threat to the continued survival of many species of bats. One obvious example is the large-scale destruction of woodlands and forests, usually associated with human activities such as logging. In the tropics of Central and South America, species like the little big-eared bat live in relatively undisturbed forest situations, ranging from the scrub forest of the Yucatán Peninsula in Mexico to the more spectacular rain forest that is widespread in much of South America. These bats, like other species of the forest, are quick to disappear when their habitat is disturbed. In the forests of Washington, Oregon, British Columbia, and Alberta, studies of bats have demonstrated that older stands of trees provide essential roosting opportunities for bats, which may forage in adjacent disturbed areas where logging has taken place. The impact of logging depends upon the scale of the operation and the sizes of the areas used by the bats. California myotis, at 5 grams, have smaller home ranges than big brown bats, which live in the same area and might have more difficulty surviving large-scale logging operations than the larger species.

Conservation issues can present our species with many difficult decisions, often because we are or have been responsible for the situations that develop and require action. One example of such a dilemma is provided by efforts to protect African elephants, initiatives that have received worldwide support. One immediate problem is the impact that elephants can have on woodlands, which are critical to the survival of many other species of animals and plants.

African elephants were once widespread in Africa, and today it is esti-

The lesser yellow house bat (15 grams), a species that roosts in hollow trees across much of southern Africa. This insectivore is one of the most common species in Miombo woodlands.

An eastern pipistrelle (7 grams) emerging from a hollow tree. Bats must use existing openings to gain access to hollows because their teeth and claws are too small to be used to make new openings. This insectivore is common in eastern North America.

mated that over 500,000 individuals remain in the wild. In some parts of Africa, elephant populations have been decimated by the demand for their ivory, while elsewhere on the continent they continue to flourish. Today in some parts of Zimbabwe, for example, the elephant populations are increasing at the same rate as the human populations (5 percent per year), and one habitat, the Miombo or *Brachystegia* woodlands, is caught between two destructive forces associated with these population increases. On one side, increasing elephant populations mean higher levels of tree loss directly from elephant feeding, and indirectly through the attacks of insects that exploit the damage done by the elephants. On the other side, expanding human populations mean an increased demand for firewood and land for growing crops.

There are high elephant population densities and devastated woodlands in national parks such as Matusadona and Mana Pools, while the adjacent communal lands have few elephants and intact woodlands. While many of the species of birds that are found only in this woodland have disappeared from the devastated woodlands, the common bats remain, albeit at lower population levels than in the intact woodland.

What is more important? Conserving the elephants or the woodlands and the species that depend upon them? For the time being, those that focus on saving elephants appear to have the upper hand.

OPPORTUNISM AND GOOD NEWS

The opportunism of bats does provide good news stories for conservation. Their quest for secure roosts that provide favorable conditions of temperature and humidity means that many species often roost in buildings. Before buildings were common, I suspect that many species of bat roosted in hollows in

A notch-eared bat (7 grams), which occurs widely in Europe and south into the northern part of Israel. This insectivorous species often roosts in buildings in Europe.

trees. In many parts of the world, extensive logging operations, whether for building or for agriculture, have reduced the numbers of available roosts and prompted some species of bats to move into buildings. Species like notch-eared bats often form nursery colonies in buildings in parts of Europe, but in Israel, this same species is not known to roost in buildings. Along the Golan Heights, however, these and other species of bats do roost in disused military bunkers.

In Africa, large slit-faced bats and Egyptian slit-faced bats roost in hollow acacia trees along the Zambezi River. Furthermore, some radio-tagged large slit-faced bats readily moved between the hollow trees, the support for an old water tower, and old military bunkers. Throughout the world, from Europe to North America, from Africa to India, many species of bats readily exploit artificial structures as roosts, while others do not use these locations.

The opportunism of bats is not limited to roosts. Bats also exploit the feeding opportunities generated by human activity. One of the most obvious of these is the tendency of common vampire bats to feed on the blood of cattle and other domestic animals. But human activities also generate feeding opportunities for other bats. In southern England, serotines often feed over new-mown fields, while greater horseshoe bats hunt dung beetles associated with cattle. In Germany, radio-tagged noctules often hunted over dumps, exploiting the insects attracted there. Almost everywhere, many insectivorous bats hunt in the clouds of insects attracted to streetlights.

Therefore, many species of bats benefit from the roosting and foraging opportunities presented by many of the activities of humans. One colony of notch-eared bats living in the south of Germany roosted in a church attic, which provided very good conditions for bearing and rearing young. For this colony, the flies that accumulated in a nearby cattle barn made it a good foraging stop as the bats headed out for their nightly activity.

Bats offer us excellent examples of the complexities involved in the interactions between humans and other organisms. Most bats have no impact on the lives of most humans and remain unnoticed. In spite of this generally neutral situation, bats are often persecuted largely because of our ignorance about them. The challenge to us is to find a strategy that permits other species of organisms to flourish in the face of our expectations for economic gain. Conservation is an area where practicality and idealism can collide, and bats sometimes are at the center of these collisions.

Trident leaf-nosed bats roosting in an abandoned military bunker on the Golan Heights in Israel. This insectivorous species reaches the northern limit of its distribution in Israel.

SEVEN

WHERE DO WE GO FROM HERE?

The silhouette of this gigantic flying fox embodies some of the mystery of bats.

Bats offer wonderful opportunities for further research. Although we know much more about them now than we did when Spallanzani or even Griffin began their studies, each new discovery about bats seems to generate more questions. While this may seem like a weak rationale intended to keep bat biologists busy, in learning about bats we also learn more about ourselves. Now I can reflect on two of the topics that I think will prove to be exciting for bat biologists over the next few years.

VISION

First is the role that vision plays in the lives of bats. We often speak of someone with poor vision as being "as blind as a bat," and it is easy to think that bats are

blind. They are small animals and in bright light they often have their eyes closed. Furthermore, why should animals with echolocation bother with vision?

The truth is quite different. Although relatively little work has been done on the vision of bats, we know that some species see very well. California leaf-nosed bats, for example, see as well as humans, and better than we do in dim light. All of the flying foxes and their relatives, the bats in the family Pteropodidae, have excellent vision, but most of them do not use echolocation.

Species such as Midas' free-tailed bats have large, conspicuous eyes and, as far as we can tell, excellent echolocation. Furthermore, when hunting, these bats fly high above the tree canopy in situations where they might use vision. Watching them as they hunt, and listening to their echolocation calls, suggests that in this situation they use echolocation. What do these bats do when their eyes tell them one thing and their echolocation something different? How does the bat's brain assemble a picture of the surroundings using two quite different sets of information?

I suspect that echolocation provides bats that hunt airborne targets with more dependable information about flying insects than vision. This leads to the prediction that even when hunting in bright light such bats will use echolocation. Studies of northern bats in northern Sweden support this prediction. The challenge is to extend the work to other species and find a reliable way to get bats to tell us how they see and hear the world.

These pale spear-nosed bats (40 grams) were caught in the same net in Costa Rica. As far as we know they belong to the same species but represent different color variations. Other species of bats, including lesser bulldog bats, show similar variations in color. The significance of the variations remains unclear. This fruit-eating species occurs widely in South and Central America.

What role does color play in the lives of bats? The microchiropteran bats are thought to be color-blind, and yet female eastern red bats are much more drab in color than males. What is the behavioral significance of this difference in appearance? We do not know. How well do yellow-shouldered bats see the glandular areas of sexually mature males? Some species of bats show distinct color varieties. The two pale spear-nosed bats on the previous page, so strikingly different in color, were taken in the same mist net in Costa Rica. Questions about what bats see have implications for other aspects of their lives.

A COLONY OF BATS

Too often throughout this book I have spoken of a "colony" of bats. What do I mean? The simplest interpretation would be that the colony is the bats that are together when I encounter them. But are the members of a group of bats that I find in a roost really a cohesive unit, or are they like the people coming out of a high-rise building? They may live under the same roof but have little else in common and nothing much to do with one another. Using this definition of a colony would mean concluding that bats are not particularly social animals. Gregarious yes, social no.

But I also mentioned experimental evidence suggesting that the little brown bats and big brown bats that roost together in a building (a colony) have similar echolocation calls. This means that if you analyze the calls of bats from several different roosts and ask a computer to sort the bats, it will arrange them by colony. This evidence, coupled with the reality that individual bats may return year after year to the same roost, implies that there is more to a colony of big brown or little brown bats than just gregariousness. For the time being, we need to pursue the subject and learn more about the decisions that bats make in their selection of roosts and roost mates.

Common vampire bats are much more than gregarious. In this species the members of a colony may, on any night, use several different roosts. The colony members do not always roost together, and yet the bat that comes home without having fed can beg blood from one of its successful roost mates. Work in Costa Rica shows that these bats will regurgitate blood to roost mates and that the roost mates are not all genetically related. The "society" of common vampire bats provides a social safety net for colony members. There are obvious benefits to the individual that belongs to such an organization.

I am certain that in some cases a "colony" of bats is a cohesive social unit in which the members "know" one another. It also seems clear that in other cases the group of bats at a feeding or roosting site may be just an aggregation. Furthermore, for any one species different groupings of bats may be social structures while others are not. When it comes to defining a social unit, bats may prove to have a good deal in common with humans.

A CLASSIFICATION
OF BATS

A † denotes those species known only as fossils.

Order Chiroptera
    Megachiropteramorpha
        suborder Megachiroptera
            Family Pteropodidae, the Old World fruit bats (flying foxes) and their relatives
    Microchiropteramorpha
        Family Icaronycteridae †
        Family Archaeonycteridae †
    Microchiropteraformes
        Family Palaeochiropterygidae †
        Family Hassianycteridae †

suborder Microchiroptera

    superfamily Emballonuroidea

        Family Emballonuridae, the sheath-tailed bats

Infraorder Yinochiroptera

    superfamily Rhinopomatoidea

        Family Craseonycteridae, the bumblebee bats

        Family Rhinopomatidae, the mouse-tailed bats

    superfamily Rhinolophoidea

        Family Nycteridae, the slit-faced bats

        Family Megadermatidae, the false vampire bats

        Family Rhinolophidae, the horseshoe bats

        Family Hipposideridae, the Old World leaf-nosed bats

Infraorder Yangochiroptera

        Family Philididae †

        Family Mystacinidae, the short-tailed bats

    superfamily Noctilionoidea

        Family Phyllostomidae, the New World leaf-nosed bats

        Family Mormoopidae, the moustache bats

        Family Noctilionidae, the bulldog bats

    superfamily Nataloidea

        Family Myzopodidae, the Old World sucker-footed bats

        Family Thyropteridae, the New World sucker-footed bats

        Family Furipteridae, the thumbless bats

Family Natalidae, the funnel-eared bats
superfamily Molossoidea
Family Antrozoidae, the pallid bats
Family Molossidae, the free-tailed bats
superfamily Vespertilionoidea
Family Vespertilionidae, the plain-nosed bats

BAT ANATOMY

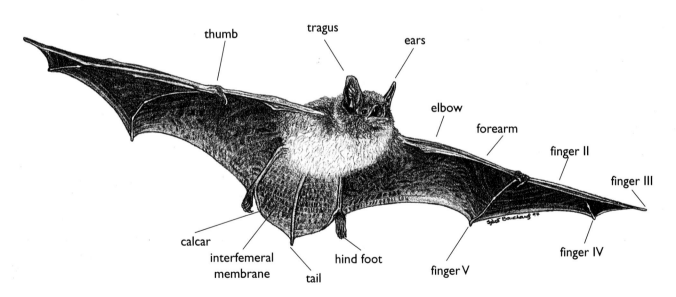

thumb

tragus

ears

elbow

forearm

finger II

finger III

calcar

interfemeral membrane

tail

hind foot

finger V

finger IV

Drawing by Sylvie Bouchard

COMMON AND SCIENTIFIC NAMES OF BATS

The + denotes species illustrated in this book.

COMMON NAME	SCIENTIFIC NAME	FAMILY
Bent-winged bats	Miniopterus species	Vespertilionidae
Big brown bat+	Eptesicus fuscus	Vespertilionidae
Big-eared brown bat+	Histiotus velatus	Vespertilionidae
Bodenheimer's pipistrelle+	Pipistrellus bodenheimeri	Vespertilionidae
Brown long-eared bat	Plecotus auritus	Vespertilionidae
Bulldog bats	Noctilio species	Noctilionidae
Bumblebee bat	Craseonycteris thonglongyai	Craseonycteridae
California leaf-nosed bat+	Macrotus californicus	Phyllostomidae

COMMON NAME	SCIENTIFIC NAME	FAMILY
California myotis+	Myotis californicus	Vespertilionidae
Cape serotine+	Eptesicus capensis	Vespertilionidae
Common free-tailed bat+	Eumops auripendulus	Molossidae
Common vampire bat+	Desmodus rotundus	Phyllostomidae
Club-footed bats	Tylonycteris species	Vespertilionidae
Davy's naked-backed bat+	Pteronotus davyii	Mormoopidae
Eastern pipistrelle+	Pipistrellus subflavus	Vespertilionidae
Eastern red bat+	Lasiurus borealis	Vespertilionidae
Eastern small-footed bat	Myotis leibii	Vespertilionidae
Egyptian fruit bat+	Rousettus aegyptiacus	Pteropodidae
Egyptian slit-faced bat+	Nycteris thebaica	Nycteridae
Epauletted fruit bat+	Epomophorus wahlbergi	Pteropodidae
European free-tailed bat	Tadarida teniotis	Molossidae
False vampire bats		Megadermatidae
Fishing bats	Myotis species	Vespertilionidae
Flying foxes+		Pteropodidae
Fringe-lipped bat	Trachops cirrhosus	Phyllostomidae
Fringed myotis+	Myotis thysanodes	Vespertilionidae
Funnel-eared bat+	Natalus stramineus	Natalidae
Geoffroy's horseshoe bat+	Rhinolophus clivosus	Rhinolophidae
Gigantic flying fox	Pteropus giganteus	Pteropodidae
Gray long-eared bat+	Plecotus austriacus	Vespertilionidae

COMMON NAME	SCIENTIFIC NAME	FAMILY
Greater bulldog bat+	Noctilio leporinus	Noctilionidae
Greater horseshoe bat	Rhinolophus ferrumequinum	Rhinolophidae
Greater spear-nosed bat	Phyllostomus hastatus	Phyllostomidae
Hairy-legged vampire bat	Diphylla ecaudata	Phyllostomidae
Hemprich's big-eared bat+	Otonycteris hemprichi	Vespertilionidae
Hoary bat+	Lasiurus cinereus	Vespertilionidae
Horseshoe bats	Rhinolophus species	Rhinolophidae
Indian false vampire bat	Megaderma lyra	Megadermatidae
Intermediate fruit bat+	Artibeus intermedius	Phyllostomidae
Jamaican fruit bat+	Artibeus jamaicensis	Phyllostomidae
Kuhl's pipistrelle+	Pipistrellus kuhlii	Vespertilionidae
Large slit-faced bat+	Nycteris grandis	Nycteridae
Lesser bulldog bat+	Noctilio albiventris	Noctilionidae
Lesser yellow house bat	Scotophilus borbonicus	Vespertilionidae
Lesser spear-nosed bat+	Phyllostomus discolor	Phyllostomidae
Linnaeus' false vampire bat+	Vampyrum spectrum	Phyllostomidae
Little big-eared bat+	Micronycteris megalotis	Phyllostomidae
Little brown bat+	Myotis lucifugus	Vespertilionidae
Little free-tailed bat+	Tadarida pumila	Molossidae
Little sac-winged bat+	Peropteryx macrotis	Emballonuridae
Long-tailed serotine+	Eptesicus hottentotus	Vespertilionidae
Malaysian free-tailed bat+	Tadarida mops	Molossidae

COMMON NAME	SCIENTIFIC NAME	FAMILY
Martienssen's free-tailed bat+	Otomops martiensseni	Molossidae
Mauritian tomb bat+	Taphozous mauritianus	Emballonuridae
Mexican free-tailed bat	Tadarida brasiliensis	Molossidae
Mexican long-tongued bat+	Choeronycteris mexicana	Phyllostomidae
Midas' free-tailed bat	Tadarida midas	Molossidae
Mouse-eared bats	Myotis species	Vespertilionidae
New World leaf-nosed bats		Phyllostomidae
Noack's leaf-nosed bat+	Hipposideros caffer	Hipposideridae
Noctule+	Nyctalus noctula	Vespertilionidae
Northern bat	Eptesicus nilssoni	Vespertilionidae
Northern long-eared bat+	Myotis septentrionalis	Vespertilionidae
Notch-eared bat+	Myotis emarginatus	Vespertilionidae
Old World leaf-nosed bats		Hipposideridae
Pale spear-nosed bat+	Phyllostomus discolor	Phyllostomidae
Pallid bat	Antrozous pallidus	Antrozoidae
Parnell's moustached bat+	Pteronotus parnellii	Mormoopidae
Peters bat+	Balantiopteryx plicata	Emballonuridae
Plain-nosed bats		Vespertilionidae
Proboscis bat+	Rhynchonycteris naso	Emballonuridae
Pygmy fruit bat+	Artibeus phaeotis	Phyllostomidae
Red mastiff bat+	Molossus ater	Molossidae
Schmidt's large-eared bat+	Micronycteris schmidtorum	Phyllostomidae

COMMON NAME	SCIENTIFIC NAME	FAMILY
Schreiber's bent-winged bat+	Miniopterus schreibersii	Vespertilionidae
Serotine	Eptesicus serotinus	Vespertilionidae
Sheath-tailed bats		Emballonuridae
Short-nosed fruit bat+	Cynopterus brachyotis	Pteropodidae
Short-tailed fruit bat+	Carollia perspicillata	Phyllostomidae
Silver-haired bat+	Lasionycteris noctivagans	Vespertilionidae
Slit-faced bats	Nycteris species	Nycteridae
Small long-faced bat+	Anoura caudifer	Phyllostomidae
Smoky bat+	Furipterus horrens	Furipteridae
Spotted bat	Euderma maculatum	Vespertilionidae
Tome's long-eared bat+	Lonchorhina aurita	Phyllostomidae
Trident leaf-nosed bat+	Asellia tridens	Hipposideridae
Western big-eared bat+	Plecotus townsendii	Vespertilionidae
Western small-footed bat	Myotis ciliolabrum	Vespertilionidae
Whitehead's fruit bat+	Harpyionycteris whiteheadi	Pteropodidae
White-winged vampire bat	Diaemus youngi	Phyllostomidae
Woermann's bat+	Megaloglossus woermanni	Pteropodidae
Wood's slit-faced bat+	Nycteris woodii	Nycteridae
Yellow-shouldered bat+	Sturnira lilium	Phyllostomidae
Yellow-winged bat+	Lavia frons	Megadermatidae

OTHER BOOKS ABOUT BATS

Allen, G. M. 1939. *Bats*. Harvard University Press, Cambridge.

Altringham, J. D. 1996. *Bats: Biology and Behaviour*. Oxford University Press, London.

Barbour, R. W. and W. H. Davis. 1969. *Bats of America*. University of Kentucky Press, Lexington.

Barclay, R. M. R. and R. M. Brigham (editors). 1996. *Bats and Forests Symposium*, October 19–21, 1995, Victoria, British Columbia. B.C. Ministry of Forests, Victoria.

Brosset, A. 1966. *La biologie des chiroptères*. Masson et Cie, Paris.

Busnel, R-G. and J. F. Fish (editors). 1980. *Animal Sonar Systems*. Plenum Press, New York.

Fenton, M. B. 1983. *Just Bats*. University of Toronto Press, Toronto.

Fenton, M. B. 1985. *Communication in the Chiroptera*. University of Indiana Press, Bloomington.

Fenton, M. B. 1992. *Bats*. Facts on File Inc., New York.

Fenton, M. B., P. A. Racey, and J. M. V. Rayner (editors). 1987. *Recent Advances in the Study of Bats*. Cambridge University Press, Cambridge.

Findley, J. S. 1993. *Bats: A Community Perspective*. Cambridge University Press, Cambridge.

Fleming, T. H. 1988. *The Short-tailed Fruit Bat*. University of Chicago Press, Chicago.

Greenhall, A. M. and U. Schmidt (editors). 1988. *Natural History of*

Vampire Bats. CRC Press Inc., Boca Raton.

Griffin, D. R. 1958. *Listening in the Dark*. Yale University Press, New Haven (reprinted in 1986 by Comstock/Cornell).

Hanak, V., I. Horacek, and J. Gaisler (editors). 1989. *European Bat Research 1987*. Charles University Press, Prague.

Hill, J. E. and J. D. Smith. 1985. *Bats: A Natural History*. British Museum (Natural History), London.

Kunz, T. H. (editor). 1982. *Ecology of Bats*. Plenum Press, New York.

Kunz, T. H. (editor). 1988. *Ecological and Behavioral Methods for the Study of Bats*. Smithsonian Press, Washington.

Leen, N. and A. Novick. 1969. *The World of Bats*. Holt Rinehart and Winston, New York.

Nagorsen, D. W. and R. M. Brigham. 1993. *The Bats of British Columbia*. University of British Columbia Press, Vancouver, B.C.

Norberg, U. M. 1989. "Vertebrate flight, mechanics, physiology, morphology, ecology and evolution." *Zoophysiology* 27:1–291. Springer-Verlag, Berlin.

Pollak, G. D. and J. H. Casseday. 1989. "The neural basis of echolocation in bats." *Zoophysiology* 25:1–143. Springer-Verlag, Berlin.

Popper, A. N. and R. R. Fay (editors). 1995. *Hearing by Bats*. Springer-Verlag, New York.

Racey, P. A. and S. M. Swift (editors). 1995. *Ecology, Evolution and Behaviour of Bats*. Symposia of the Zoological Society of London no. 67. Clarendon Press, Oxford.

Ransome, R. 1990. *The Natural History of Hibernating Bats*. Christopher Helm, London.

Richarz, K. and A. Limbrunner. 1993. *The World of Bats*. T.F.H. Publications, Neptune City, NJ.

Robertson, J. *The Complete Bat*. Chattus and Windus, London.

Roeder, K. D. 1967. *Nerve Cells and Insect Behavior*, revised edition. Harvard University Press, Cambridge.

Sales, G. and D. Pye. 1974. *Ultrasonic Communication by Animals*. Chapman and Hall, London.

Schmidly, D. J. 1991. *The Bats of Texas*. Texas A & M University Press, College Station.

Schober, W. 1984. *The Lives of Bats*. Arco Publishing Corp., New York.

Tupinier, D. 1989. *La chauve-souris et l'homme*. Editions L'Harmattan, Paris.

Turner, D. C. 1975. *The Vampire Bat: A Field Study in Behavior and Ecology*. Johns Hopkins Press, Baltimore.

Tuttle, M. D. 1988. *America's Neighborhood Bats*. University of Texas Press, Austin.

van Zyll de Jong, C. G. 1985. *Handbook of Canadian mammals. 2. Bats*. National Museums of Canada, Ottawa.

Wilson, D. E. 1997. *Bats in Question: The Smithsonian Answer Book*. Smithsonian Institution Press, Washington.

Wimsatt, W. A. (editor). 1970, 1970, 1977. *Biology of Bats*, Volumes 1, 2, and 3. Academic Press, New York.

Yalden, D. W. and P. A. Morris. 1975. *The Lives of Bats*. Quadrangle/New York Times Press, London.

FURTHER READING: SOME TECHNICAL REFERENCES

The Lure of Bats

Fenton, M. B., I. L. Rautenbach, S. E. Smith, C. M. Swanepoel, J. Grosell, and J. van Jaarsveld. 1994. "Raptors and bats: threats and opportunities." *Animal Behaviour* 48:9–18.

Bats Can See with Their Ears!

Balcombe, J. P. and M. B. Fenton. 1988. "Eavesdropping by bats: the influence of echolocation call design and foraging strategy." *Ethology* 79:158–166.

Bogdanowicz, W., R. D. Csada, and M. B. Fenton. 1997. "Noseleaf structure, echolocation and foraging behavior in the Phyllostomidae (Chiroptera)." *Journal of Mammalogy* 78:942–953.

Fenton, M. B., D. Audet, M. K. Obrist, and J. Rydell. 1995. "Signal strength, timing and self-deafening: the evolution of echolocation in bats." *Paleobiology* 21:229–242.

Surviving the Day: Where Bats Roost

Brigham, R. M. and M. B. Fenton. 1987. "The effect of roost sealing as a method to control maternity colonies of big brown bats." *Canadian Journal of Public Health* 78:47–50.

The Appearance of Bats

Fenton, M. B. 1992. "Wounds and the origin of blood-feeding in bats." *Biological Journal of the Linnean Society* 47:161–171.

Obrist, M., M. B. Fenton, J. L. Eger, and P. Schlegel. 1993. "What ears do for bats: a comparative study of pinna sound pressure transformation in Chiroptera." *Journal of Experimental Biology* 180:119–152.

The Conservation of Bats

Cumming, D. H. M., M. B. Fenton, I. L. Rautenbach, R. D. Taylor, G. S. Cumming, M. S. Cumming, J. M. Dunlop, A. G. Ford, M. D. Hovorka, D. S. Johnston, M. C. Kalcounis, Z. Mahlangu, and C. V. Portfors. 1997. "Elephant impacts on biodiversity of Miombo woodlands in Zimbabwe." *South African Journal of Science* 93:131–236.

Fenton, M. B. 1997. "Science and the conservation of bats." *Journal of Mammalogy* 78:1–14.

Fenton, M. B., L. Acharya, D. Audet, M. B. C. Hickey, C. Merriman, M. K. Obrist, D. M. Syme, and B. Adkins. 1992. "Phyllostomid bats (Chiroptera: Phyllostomidae) as indicators of habitat disruption in the neotropics." *Biotropica* 24:440–446.

Fenton, M. B., D. H. M. Cumming, I. L. Rautenbach, G. S. Cumming, M. S. Cumming, A. G. Ford, R. D. Taylor, J. M. Dunlop, M. D. Hovorka, D. S. Johnston, C. V. Portfors, M. C. Kalcounis, and Z. Mahlangu. "Bats and the loss of tree canopy in African woodlands." *Conservation Biology*, accepted March 1997.

Where Do We Go from Here?

Pearl, D. L. and M. B. Fenton. 1996. "Echolocation calls provide information about group identity in the little brown bat, *Myotis lucifugus*." *Canadian Journal of Zoology* 74:2184–2192.

ACKNOWLEDGMENTS

As in other scientific disciplines, people and money are two essential ingredients in the study of biology. It is a pleasure to thank many colleagues for discussions about bats. Lalita Acharya, John Altringham, Doris Audet, Robert Barclay, Wieslaw Bogdanowicz, Mark Brigham, Judith Eger, Mark Engstrom, James Fullard, Brian Hickey, Dave Johnston, Gareth Jones, Tom Kunz, Gary McCracken, Ulla Norberg, Martin Obrist, Christine Portfors, Naas Rautenbach, Jens Rydell, Nancy Simmons, John Speakman, Don Thomas, Jane Waterman, Melanie Watt, John Whitaker, and Gerry Wilkinson are prominent on my list of people to thank. Students are another vital group because by their questions, comments, and their own research, they have broadened and continue to expand my view of bats. I am grateful to Sylvie Bouchard, Jenna Dunlop, Brenna Forester, Samantha Kassels, Bill Scully, Jason Taylor, and Maarten Vonhof, graduate students currently working with me.

My research on bats has been generously supported by Research and Equipment Grants from NSERC, the Natural Sciences and Engineering Research Council of Canada. The research also has been supported by the Chautauqua Bird, Tree and Garden Club, by the Elsa Wild Animal Appeal, and by World Wildlife Fund (Canada).

I also thank people who helped with field work that permitted me to take some of the photographs included in this book. In Brazil, Lu Aguiar, Julio Baumgarten, Deborah Faria, Wagner Pedro, and Marlon Zortea made our trip possible. In Mexico, Hector Arita and Jorge Ortega obtained the necessary permits and worked with us in the field as did David Cumming and Russell Taylor in Zimbabwe. In Israel, Benny Shalmon, Yoram Yomtov, and Andres Mercer introduced me to many bats and study sites.

Jenna Dunlop, Henry Howden, Bill Scully, and Maarten Vonhof kindly allowed me to use some of their photographs, and Sylvie Bouchard made the drawing that shows the parts of a bat. Sylvie Bouchard, Wieslaw Bogdanowicz, Jenna Dunlop, Eleanor Fenton, Bill Scully, Maarten Vonhof, and Jane Waterman read all or parts of the manuscript and offered comments that improved it.

I also thank the bats, all of them.

INDEX